Successful, Single, But...

Nine ways to finding the man of your dreams and to keep love and happiness in your life.

Linton Claude Samuels

Copyright © 2018 ClaudeSam
All rights reserved.
ISBN-13: 978-0692130193
ISBN-10: 0692130195

*To Brenda Connie Taylor-
You will always be in my heart and in my mind.*

CONTENTS

1*	LOVE	3
2*	AVAILABILITY	33
3*	FEAR	57
4*	CHANGING	85
5*	TRADITIONS	103
6*	SPEAK UP	125
7*	PARENTS	159
8*	WALLS	179
9*	BURN IT	203
10*	CONCLUSION	229
11*	AUTHOR BIO	240

Linton Claude Samuels

ACKNOWLEDGMENTS

Writing a book is like setting off on a long journey. And like all great adventures, it is best undertaken with friends and loved ones by your side. I would like to thank the following for their gracious help and contributions to this book:

Andrew L. Nangle gave me a book that inspired me to try writing one myself. Andrew is the first friend I met when I came to the United States. He is still my good friend to this day, and I consider him a brother.

Timothy A. Julien has been a true friend and a brother to me over the years. He encouraged me to follow through and complete this book. He's been with me through my ups and downs, and I cannot thank him enough for his support and friendship.

My sisters, Diedrean P. Patton and Diedre P. Michel, have always been there for me. After the passing of our mother, they encouraged me to stay focused on my dreams and goals. They raised me and cared for me, and they both became mother figures in my life. I am eternally grateful for the love they have given to me. I am so happy to share this wonderful life with them, and know that they have my back.

Ms. Stephanie Miluso RN and her cousin Mr. Martin Keane very kindly devoted their time and passion to this project as my editors. I am indebted to them for seeing this book's potential, and for helping me to make it shine.

And finally, to my readers… thank you for deciding to read this book. I truly appreciate it. I did my best to speak to you honestly, from my heart. I hope you find my words helpful, and I wish you nothing but love and happiness on your own journeys through life. THANK YOU

INTRODUCTION

I came across this amazing quote by Grace Hopper that states, "A ship in port is safe, but that's not what ships are built for." This is so true. Ships were built for the deep blue sea. Not to be tied up at the port. When I thought about this quote, it made me think about this book I had to write. This book was meant to share with the world so people could learn the ideas that are in my head. My book was not given to me for me only. I knew that I had a message that could not only help women, but also potentially have an impact on this world.

I have thought about writing this book for a very long time, but fear and doubt were chains that held me back from pursuing my goal. I did not know how to begin to write this book until a good friend of mine, Andrew L. Nangle, a guy I consider a brother, drove to my house and gave me a book to read. About a year ago he gave me a book on faith. However, this book spoke about men and how they should live for their families and for God. I was a little skeptical at first, but his excitement propelled me to dive in the book and see what the excitement was all about.

The book was titled "How God Makes Men," by Patrick Morley. After reading a few paragraphs, I found it difficult to put the book down. I was completely hooked. Patrick Morley was not trying to tell men what they should or should not do. However, he came from a different approach. He used true stories to make his point clear. With this approach, it allowed me to not only agree with what he was saying, but moreover, it forced me to think for myself. It helped me personalize the situation from his stories which resulted with me making a decision to live the life that a Christian man should live, rather than living a life that I was told to live. This was a great strategy. I believe that his book not only changed my life, however, it helped me to think for myself. His approach to conveying his message was excellent.

For example, rather than telling someone who is obese to start exercising and changing their bad eating habits is the only way to lose weight, Patrick Morley would approach this from a different angle. He would tell you a true story about a man that was once obese and was eating himself to death until he was on his deathbed with a handful of diet related diseases. Having to witness his family and friends suffer because he was not going to live to take care of them, he decided, on that day, to change his life, so he could live and be around to take care of his family.

He started to eat healthfully. He began to cut out the fried chicken and instead, he would bake his chicken. He replaced rice and bread with a lot of leafy vegetables. He made the change from beer and soda to water. When he was strong enough to get back on his feet, he gradually walked a few steps a day until he was able to walk a mile and more a day. He lost a lot of weight and was once again a healthy man, a healthy father and a healthy parent. He was able to rid himself of all diet related diseases such as obesity, diabetes and high blood pressure.

As you can see, telling someone a story like this would be more beneficial to them to start changing their lives rather than telling them to change their diet and start exercising because they are obese. This kind of approach can have the potential to make an individual think for him or herself rather than simply doing what they are told. It is not always what you say, it is how you go about saying what it is that you have to say. This kind of approach is what I used to write this book. "Successful, Single, But...," was written to shed light on why there so many successful single women in the world that find it difficult to find a spouse or to keep their spouses in their lives.

There are many reasons that are keeping love away from many women. However, I believe it was best to focus on what women can control versus what they cannot control. Relationships are like the seasons. No one can control the seasons. In the winter season, it will be snowing, and the temperature will drop. In the rainy season, it will rain consistently. In the summer season, the temperature will rise due to the long hours of sunlight. Since we cannot control it, then we have to prepare ourselves and learn how to live our lives during these seasons. This is the same with relationships where you have the good times and the bad times, the sad times and the happy times. The times when you are fully aware of what is going on in your relationship and the times when you are completely confused and clueless as to where your relationship is going. This book was written to give you ideas on what you can do in any situation that you face in your relationship or when searching to find the spouse of your dreams.

Thus, I came up with nine reasons that could possibly eliminate or lower the rate of single successful women that are rising in this world. I must make it clear that some of my reasons may not apply to everyone, but if you find one that does apply to you then you should put it to use right away. This book is not a cure all. I believe that it does not matter how intelligent we are, we can still be ignorant to certain things and behaviors. No one is a know-it-all. Please, when reading this book, you should do so with an open mind. There are nine chapters to this book. I believe with all positives that if someone were to apply at least one chapter to their relationship, they could see a huge change for the better in their lives.

Let the chapters begin!!!

Linton Claude Samuels

Chapter 1
TRUE LOVE

> "I will love me for you, while you love you for me.
> So together we may love each other. For love is
> From within to give, with room to receive."
> -Linton Claude Samuels

One of the biggest reasons for the massive increase in the number of single women has to do with the media and the entertainment industry. The television, the magazines, the TV shows, the movies, the talk shows, I believe, are all main causes of this epidemic. Companies do and say whatever it takes to keep us buying their products and also create shows that will peak the interest of the viewers to tune in to watch their programs. I am not against television programs. I am however, against some of their messages that can intentionally damage the minds of the viewers.

I once saw a major celebrity post on Instagram. She posted a picture of her wearing a Prada bag and Prada shoes. Nothing is wrong with wearing nice things. I am all about wearing the best. Here is the issue, on the bottom of the post she wrote, "thank you Prada for giving me this gift. I love it." Although she is considered to be wealthy with a net worth that surpasses $100 million, she did not pay for the Prada bag or shoes. They were given to her as a gift. It was a free gift. Yet, when the public sees her, they try to copy their lives after hers. They try their very best to live up to that standard of living. By doing that, they work themselves to death just to keep up with that image. Is that a real image? Is this an ideal life?

The answer to those questions is no. Companies at times tend to use celebrities as walking poster boards. Sometimes the stars will actually come out and say it. These famous A-list stars are highly decorated with products that millions of people would not have seen if it were not for their star status. Take the Oscar's for example. The main reason for this event is to award actors, actresses, writers and producers for their work in Hollywood. With that said, the Oscar's is basically an award ceremony for Hollywood. So, you would think that the ceremony would be the main event right, but no it is not.

The main show is the pre-show, also known as The Red-Carpet Event. This is where all the stars show-case their attire to reporters and to the public while walking on the red carpet which leads to the entrance of the ceremony. All the A-list stars show up for this event. The cameras follow them from the time that they arrive in their limousine, to them taking pictures and answering questions, to them sitting in their seats and capturing them while they accept their awards. The reporters who meet these stars on the red carpet ask them a series of questions.

You would think that the questions had to do with the main fact that they were nominated and possibly be able to take home such a competitive award, but no. These are not the main questions. The main questions are, "What are you wearing?" "Who are you wearing?" "Why did you choose to wear that brand?" "Where did you get your necklace?" "You smell amazing, what perfume are you wearing and why did you choose that scent?" The stars then answer the questions. For every answer, the brands are directly being advertised to the public. From this, sales can in fact increase and the brand will become either more popular or if it's a new brand in the market, it can be known because of the great event called The Red Carpet.

In the year 2005, Chris Rock hosted the Oscars. His job was to host the event and do it in such a way that he could make people laugh. Come on, he is a phenomenal comedian. He walked on the stage, took the mic and right away, he acknowledged how handsome and sexy he looked in his suit. Then put the mic to his mouth and thanked P. Diddy for giving him his tuxedo. P. Diddy brand is Sean John. At the time, I did not think about purchasing a Sean John suit. Maybe I did not know that P. Diddy made suits. Well, I know now.

Just from the Red-Carpet Event alone, the average person would go shopping to look as elegant as the A-list stars. They would work a second job, work overtime or pursue careers that could potentially afford them the celebrity lifestyle. The most sickening option I find is when the hunger to live a life like a television personality is so strong that it makes you go searching for a spouse who could give you that type of lifestyle. This is not what life is like in the real world. The average person does not make $10 million annually. The average person does not have a net worth of $50 million. Also, the average person does not get free hand bags, free four-inch-heels or even a free

$30,000 dress. The average person has to work for everything he has. Nothing is given for free in the real world. The entertainment industry is all about marketing and entertainment. It is just about putting a face to a product. Trying to keep up with such a life will just keep you miserable. The average person cannot afford a celebrity life. Yet, that life is pursued.

I am the type of guy that will indirectly interview women without them knowing. I really like to pick their brains to understand why and how they think. I have met and spoken to many career-driven women and it pains my heart to see them struggle for love not knowing that they are the ones that are hindering their own happiness. I have met some ladies that will judge a man based on the lifestyle he can give them rather than the love he can give.

I know this sounds a bit corny, but it is the truth: Material possessions are not love. Traveling around the world and seeing major cities is not a quarter of one percent of what love is. Receiving a pair of shoes with a unique shade of red at the bottom of the shoes is not love. Your spouse buying you the best outfits that can marvel the eyes of your friends and other people is not love. Your future husband purchasing a home for you with granite countertops, top of the line stainless steel appliances, three-car garage, a master suite with his and her walk-in closets and separate his and her sinks, is not what real love is. There are people who have been given all this and a lot more, yet they are unhappy. They are unhappy because they lack the main ingredient of life and that ingredient is love.

What is love? I have searched all over to find the meaning of love. According to the dictionary, the word love means: an intense feeling of deep affection, a deep feel of romantic or sexual attachment to someone. These definitions are generally based on feelings and expressions. My favorite definition of the word love comes from the Bible, it reads:

Love is patient, Love is kind

It does not envy, it does not boast

It is not proud, it does not dishonor others

It is not self-seeking, it is not easily angered

It keeps no record of wrongs

Love does not delight in evil but rejoices with the truth

It always protects, always trust, always hopes, always perseveres.

Love never fails.

1 Corinthians 13: 4 -8 NIV

I would like you to read and digest those words. Try to understand each line. On each line, dissect every word. When you are doing this exercise, I would like you to paint a picture of the perfect spouse that you are looking for.

The first line states that love is patient love is kind. Let us take a look at the word PATIENT. Patient by definition means able to accept or tolerate delays, problems, or suffering without becoming annoyed or anxious. Ladies are princesses, goddesses, who need to be adored. The Bible went as far as to say that men should love their wives like God loves his church. Sometimes it is difficult to understand women. That is true, however ladies, you should look for men who will be patient enough to try to understand you. Although he does not get your point, if he is the guy you are looking for, he would say to himself, "she is not making any sense, but let me see where she is coming from rather than getting upset and start speaking to her like she is a piece of filth." He would continue to ask her questions so she can explain more clearly her feelings.

The second definition for love in the first line is KIND. Kindness is the quality of being friendly, generous and considerate. To be kind is to have the sense of charitableness, generosity, hospitality, compassion, concern and warm-heartedness. A person with the character of kindness is someone who possesses love in his or her heart. These individuals think about others and put them first. Someone who is kind will always value other people and make them feel worthwhile and special. A kindhearted individual is unselfish. A man who is kind would show kindness to his lady every day, every week, every month and every year till the day he dies.

 I was speaking to a friend on the phone in January 2017. She was telling me about the guy she was dating. She informed me that at times he was not kind to her. I listened to her as she opened up to me. She told me about a particular occasion where both of them were traveling back to their country. They were not traveling together. It just happened that they were heading back at the same time. According to her, he told her that he would wait for her at the airport, so they could have dinner and hangout for a bit and then travel home together. She thought that was sweet of him. When her plane landed, she could not control her emotions. She was so excited to see him and spend time with him knowing the fact that they have not seen each other for a long time. After she received her luggage at the baggage claim, she finally exited the airport. She called him to see where he was. When he finally picked up the phone, she said she was so hurt. He said that he just decided to go home and not wait anymore. That was all that he said. He did not leave for an emergency. Nothing physically had happened to give him reasons for leaving. He just changed his mind abruptly and neglected to inform her of his decision, causing her feelings to be hurt and her time to have been wasted.

She was happy to see him, yet the feeling was not mutual. My goal is to spread the news to women all over the world about how to find a spouse who will consistently treat them right. When a man is in love with a woman, he does not try to be kind. Being kind is one of the definitions of love and he will then show his kindness automatically. Kindness would be part of his nature. There would not be any room for false pretenses. His true colors will show. Kindness will show because he has true love in his heart.

To continue, the second line of the quote of love states that love does not envy, it does not boast. The definition of envy is a feeling of discontented or resentful longing aroused by someone else's possessions, qualities or luck. When someone has the character of envy in their heart, they are basically unhappy with themselves. They are unhappy with what they have and where they are in life.

Having a relationship with someone like this can really put a damper on your spirit. They are not content with their own life and they will always work extra hard to keep up with others. Worse, they would drag their finances to the ground which would lead to debt.

People with envy are always unhappy. They complain, nag and walk around with a sour face. A man who possesses envy will ignore you and your feelings. Reason being, he is so focused on making the extra dollar to have what the neighbor has. So, he spends more time at work. He uses up the credit card. He steals from you. That is not what you are looking for. Ladies, you should look for someone who can give you the attention you truly deserve. Someone who can put you and your desires first, not second or third. A man without envy in his heart is a man who is content with life. He loves life. He appreciates what he has yet he wants to be more valuable to society and his family, so he studies and works a little harder to be the man he wants to be. He does not try to keep up with what others are doing and to have what others have. All he cares about is his family and what his wife needs. His focus is all about what is important, truly important. Family is what's most important.

The second part of the second line states: love does not boast. According to the dictionary, to boast is to talk with excessive pride and self-satisfaction about one's achievements, possessions, or abilities. People with this characteristic will show off, gloat, brag, blow their own horn for people to praise them or to just feel good about themselves. When looking for a lifelong partner to love, you have to observe the individual to see if the person possesses this type of character. This character is not suitable for marriage.

I saw a TED Talks program that featured a beautiful model. The title of her talk was entitled "Looks aren't everything. Believe me, I'm a model." Before she got into her message, she did the first wardrobe change on stage. This has never happened before. She came out wearing a sexy stunning dress. Her dress was a bit on the short side. It was about a foot above her knee. She had long legs, so maybe it was the angle of the camera that made the dress seem shorter than it was. She, however, made reference to her dress being short. She looked like a goddess. She breathed sexily. "Heaven has to be real" I said to myself because I have never seen someone as beautiful as she was for a very long time. She was flawlessly perfect. She then put on a longer dress and sweater to hide all the skin that she was showing and at this point her presentation began.

I guess I was a bit naive or just ignorant about the modeling industry because almost everything she said was a surprise to me. First of all, she showed a picture of herself where she was hugging a man in very sexy way. She had her left leg around his waist and her fingers were in his hair. The man had his face very close to her neck and his right hand in her back pocket. According to her, when that photo was taken she had never had a boyfriend. She said that the photographers had to tell her exactly what she should do step by step. From how she put her legs to how she placed her hands in his hair.

In addition, she explained the ideal definition of a beautiful woman. Her definition clearly stated: tall, long shiny hair, good bone structure and a slim toned figure. She had every aspect of a beautiful lady, yet she was insecure. How could someone so beautiful be insecure? She went so far as to say that many models are insecure about themselves, that they believe they are not beautiful enough. They are slim and toned and yet they believe they are not slim enough. Although they have shiny hair, still, they think that their hair is somehow someway not shiny enough. Yes, they have good bone structure, yet they feel like their bone structure is not structured properly to express their true beauty. So, they hide their insecurities with makeup and high-end attire. The fitted dresses that never touch their knees. They hide their low self-esteem with their shiny hair that is professionally styled with multiple hair products. They cover their eyes with top-of-the-line sunglasses so no one can see how they really feel. All this is to hide their insecurities.

When someone is boastful, they tend to do the exact same thing in different ways. Like some models, a person who is a boaster tends to hide his or her insecurities with words and actions. When talking about themselves, a boaster would exaggerate the truth so the people listening would think highly of them. The boaster would overemphasize whatever it is that can bring attention to themselves. These individuals would overdo a task or overplay a simple game not only to win, but also because of their insecurities. They are empty inside and would go all out to win so they could temporarily brag and gloat about their accomplishments knowing that when they are alone they are back to being pathetic prideful individuals.

I once attended a concert at Juilliard, which is one of the top music schools in the world. I sat next to a young man about five years my senior. I was so amazed by the amount of talent I was witnessing that I could not hold back my emotions any longer. I turned to the young man and said, "this is beautiful!" He smiled, then he nodded his head up and down in agreement with me. Then suddenly two ladies walked onto the stage. I observed that one had a book in her hand and the other did not. Then suddenly, the lady that was not carrying the book went directly to the piano and sat down. The other lady with the book also walked to the piano but she did not sit down. She, however, placed the book on the piano and opened it. Her job was to turn the page of the book while the other lady played.

While they were walking towards the piano, the people in the audience stood up and gave a standing ovation. Then there was silence. The page was turned, and the room was filled with the sweet sound of music. I was just stunned. The lady playing was playing very quickly. Her fingers looked like they were barely touching the keys of the piano. At one point, I thought she was playing so fast that the lady turning the page could not keep up with her. She had great techniques. Her fingers glided up and down the piano doing multiple techniques with ease. I have never in my life seen someone play the piano like that lady.

The music was so beautiful. I too play the piano but not like that. I can only dream of becoming that good. I then turned to the young man next to me and asked him, "do you play the piano?" He replied, "yes, I am learning." He then complimented the lady playing the piano. He was as amazed by her skills as I was. While we were talking, the lady on the piano kept on playing. He then asked me if I play the piano. With my chest out and my shoulders back, smiling at him I said, "yes, I play for my church. I am my church's musician. I also play for my choir." I actually demonstrated the definition of a boastful individual. I did not know how I developed that type of attitude, but I am happy that I was able to rid myself of it.

Suddenly, the music stopped. The audience went wild. I stood up as did everyone else and applauses rang throughout the auditorium. Then something strange happened. The lady who had been playing the piano stood up and began clapping with a smile on her face while she looked in my direction. Then the audience turned around and also was smiling and clapping in my direction. I figured that they were clapping for someone behind me. So, I turned around and realized that I was wrong. I turned back around with a confused look on my face. Finally, the young man next to me stood up and waved his hands to the audience and took a bow. I turned to him and said, "why are you bowing and why are they clapping for you?" He looked at me and said, "I wrote the music the lady was playing."

I asked him earlier if he could play the piano and he said that he was learning. Yet he wrote the music for the pianist to play. I was so happy to say how good I was and how much I played at my church and he never spoke about how talented he was. He gave credit to the lady who played the music. He spoke about her and how well she was playing. He was just as amazed at her skills as I was, yet he was the composer of the music. This is what is called humility. He was humble.

Ladies, when looking for love, you have to look for someone who is humble. When someone is humble, like that composer, you will always be glorified and be placed on a pedestal in a matter of speaking. You would know that a man really loves you by how much he pays attention to every detail concerning you. He will rejoice when you succeed and despite your failures, he would make an effort to help you to look on the bright side. A man without a speck of boasting in his heart is a man who would be a possible father to your children and an amazing husband or just the perfect individual you want to have by your side. This man will not dishonor others and be self-seeking.

The next part of the love quote that I want to talk about, is the part that says, "Love is not easily angered." We are all human beings. Getting angry is a part of life. However, we have to learn how to channel that anger in a positive way. Getting angry too quickly can cause us to hurt those we care about most. Some characteristics of anger are vexation, fury, rage and wrath. How can someone express their love to you when they are constantly in a rage? Can you spend the rest of your life with someone you are afraid of? Can you walk on your tippy toes or on eggshells to avoid saying or doing the wrong thing that can cause your spouse to fly into a state of anger, knowing that your spouse is very short tempered? I hope your answer is "No" to all questions. When someone loves you, you will be able to be yourself around that person. You will be able to make mistakes knowing that your spouse understands that you are a human being and making mistakes are a part of life.

As a child growing up in Jamaica, I had a problem speaking. My stuttering was so severe that all I would do was make sounds of words rather than the words that I wanted to say. It usually took me a long time to say the simplest words. I could remember people laughing at me when I was stuttering. Sometimes I would have to stamp my feet on the ground or clap my hands to get the words out. Most people did not take me serious or even give me respect. In the late 1980's in Jamaica, teachers were allowed to discipline their students. I used to get a lot of spankings although I did nothing wrong.

I can remember this incident like it was yesterday. Something happened in my classroom and the teacher asked who did it. She went around the room with a ruler in her hands. Everyone said no immediately when they were asked the question. However, when she came to me and asked me the question, the answer could not come out of my mouth. It took me a long time to say the word "No." I did almost everything to get the word out of my mouth, but it just stayed unspoken. I kept trying. I clapped my hands, but no words came out. I stomped my feet but no words. I banged on the table and still no words. Finally, the teacher's patience ran out and she disciplined me. Her reasoning was that the fact that I was stuttering meant that I was lying.

For years things like this would happen to me. I became a bitter individual because of this. I was mad at everyone. I went from being a nice little boy to an angry one. I was not aware of how severe my anger was until I was standing in front of three police officers and listening to them speak to me like I was a criminal. At the time, I was about eight years old. The officers said many things to me that day. Only one thing that they said actually stuck with me until this day. One of the officers looked at me and said, "the next time you do this you are going to jail." Wow! His message was crystal clear.

    A few days prior to the officers showing up at my school, I did something very bad to one of my classmates. I climbed a mango tree to pick a mango. I saw only one nice juicy mango. So, I picked it. I was thinking whether or not I should eat the mango on the tree or eat it while I walked home. I decided to eat it on the way home. The tree had many thick branches and there were a few bees' nests. I needed both hands to get myself down and out of the tree. This meant that I had to throw my mango on the ground. I aimed the mango, so it could land on my book bag and I aimed it perfectly. My mango landed on my book bag safe and sound without bruising.

    Then out of the nowhere, one of my classmates walked towards the tree and picked up my mango. I tried to yell at him and tell him not to eat my mango. The words could not come out in time. My severe stuttering held my words in chains. No words came out. Then he bit my mango. Finally, I came out of the tree. My anger was fueled with indignation and outrage. All I did when I came out of the tree was to find something to hurt this mango thief. I looked down and I found a stone with a pointy end. I picked up the stone and I walked straight to him and I used the pointy end of the stone and stabbed him in his eye a few times. Sadly, he is now blind in one eye.

I felt like my action was merited, but was it? If I had love in my heart, would I have done such an awful act to someone? The answer is no to both questions. I allowed my short temper to breed anger that adulterated my judgment, which resulted in me hurting another person. If I was slow to anger, I would have let him know that he was wrong and then walked away. Let's face it, I had a helper who washed my clothes and cooked for me. My father normally would take home KFC and treats for my sisters and me. We were never in a shortage of food. If we were, I did not know because I always had food to eat. Sadly, most students at my school would only have breakfast and lunch in school. After they left school, they would go hungry until the next day at school. My father sat down and spoke to me. I was sorry for what I did. I felt sad when I saw my friend with his right eye closed permanently because of me. He was hungry, and I did not show compassion.

My stuttering was the core of my anger issues. However, that does not negate the fact that I hurt others in the process of venting my anger. It is not an excuse. I had to find out a way to control my anger, so I could be a loving individual to others. My mother bought me a piano and that piano had become my oasis. It has been my escape from hurt, pain and frustration. I learned that I have to love myself. Someone with love will not take someone else's eye sight for a mango. Someone who is quick to get angry would do something like that. Love is not easily angered. This is why parents are told that before they discipline their children for doing something wrong, they should first calm down and wait until they are relaxed before speaking to or spanking the child. Doing this will make the parents speak to their children with love while letting the children know that what they did was wrong.

So, ladies, when you are looking for that ideal spouse, make sure he is slow to anger. If he is not, then not only will he not love you, but you could be abused by him. Abuse in all its definitions is not love. A man must control his temper when addressing you. He must lower his voice when talking to you. He has to touch you gently even when you upset him. Rather than running away when a dispute occurs, he should stand his ground and resolve the issue. A man doing all of this is a man who loves his lady. His actions are saying that even though you are upsetting me, my love for you will never fail. His character should let her know that though she may have been wrong, she is still his queen and that there is nothing she can do which would cause him to love her less. Ladies, just a quick note. When a man shows love like this, do not take it lightly. This does not mean that he is weak. It means the exact opposite. It means that he is strong. Just remember this, only strong men can show love like this.

The next part of the love quote that I want to talk about is the part that reads, "Love, it keeps no record of wrongs." Theologians, pastors, priests and ministers would call this love the forgiving spirit or the forgiving character. Let us go back in biblical times when Jesus was hanging on the cross. He was beaten with whips. The flesh on His back was peeling and blood was dripping from the many lashes He received. Then, His legs and hands were tied to the cross. The Romans soldiers took nails and nailed His hands and His feet to the cross. After that, His cross was raised and it dropped down into a hole so it could stand. For some reason, the Romans were not yet finished with

Him, so they pierced His side. The movie, "The Passion of Christ," vividly portrays the moments leading to Jesus' death.

To see the pain that Jesus was enduring was really tough to watch. But then something happened. Before He died, He asked His Father to forgive them. If that were me, I would not have asked forgiveness for the soldiers and my accusers. If I were Jesus, I would have asked God to strike them down with lightning. The message that Jesus was trying to show us is that we have to forgive others who have done us wrong. We have to forgive them and put it behind us. The Lord's Prayer reads: "forgive us our debts as we forgive our debtors." Ladies, you have to find a man who lives his life according to the Lord's Prayer. You need someone to be quick to forgive you and to put your wrong-doing in the past. Forgiveness is not only for the person who has done the deed, it is also for the person against whom the deed was done. When you forgive someone, you are basically throwing the wrong-doing that they have done to you into the sea of forgiveness. Effectively wiping the slate clean and moving on as if nothing happened.

This character of love I find to be amazing. Jesus forgave his accusers and also the soldiers who had beaten Him and nailed Him to His cross. He also forgave the people who spat on Him. God forgave Abraham for having sex with Hagar, his wife's handmaid. God forgave Moses for killing an Egyptian soldier. God forgave Jacob for stealing his brother's birthright. David was forgiven after he lusted for and had sex with Uriah's wife. Uriah was a soldier in David's army. David went a step further and had Uriah placed on the front line of the battle so he would be killed. It was so, Uriah was killed. God called David "a man after My own heart." Despite all the wrongdoing these men did, they acknowledged that they made mistakes and asked for forgiveness. God forgave them all. I asked myself why did God forgive them? I found the answer: it was because He loved them.

Forgiveness is part of love. Forgiveness is in the DNA of love. If a man does not have the heart and the mind to forgive, then love is not in his heart. No one on this earth is perfect. We have all made mistakes in our lives. We probably will make more mistakes tomorrow. That is ok. Yet we still need someone to love us. After you have made a mistake, you need the comfort of knowing that your spouse loves you still. When you get home, he will embrace you the same way. He will let you know that he was hurt and ask you to not do it again. He would put your wrongdoing in the past and continue to shower you with love.

The purpose of writing this chapter is to make it known that love is a principle. It is ok to want material possessions and to travel the world, but your main focus should be about finding love, joy and happiness. Someone could give you everything you want yet you can still feel empty inside because the void in your heart is not filled. Love comes from within. Love is a light that shines out of someone. If you are with someone who is not making you experience love, based on the love quote, then it does not matter what material things, toys or physical activities you are enjoying with that individual. If there is no love, everything else will eventually fall apart. As the end of the quote states, "Love never fails."

In conclusion, I would like you to think about the story of two builders. Both builders went to the same school. Both builders were taught by the same teacher. Both builders were trained with the same chief builder. Then, both builders became well known for their building abilities. They were asked to build a house. Both agreed to start and complete the project. Builder A built his house on the sand. While builder B built his house on a rock. After both houses were completed, there was a storm. Then the sea level began to rise. The tempest wind began to whistle. You could sense the calm before the storm. Suddenly, the drizzling rain changed to heavy flowing rain. The wind increased its whistling to the roaring of a lion which had not had a kill for weeks. All of a sudden, the ocean started to make its way to dry land and destroyed everything in its path.

House A could not stand against the flood waters. The rain and the floods destroyed house A, which was built on the sand. The sand started to erode. The erosion caused the foundation of house A to weaken. Then, abruptly, the wind started to change its direction. The northwesterly winds turned into east-west winds. The east-west winds then turned to southwesterly winds. The winds kept changing directions which added pressure on the foundation of house A. Finally, house A was destroyed. The flood waters, the heavy rain and the monstrous winds were too much for house A, which had been built on sand, to withstand.

House B on the other hand, stood tall throughout the storm. The wind destroyed some of the windows which was the only evidence that a storm had passed through. House B was built on a solid foundation. A foundation that could pass any test. This foundation could withstand any disaster. Though the ocean pushed past its bank and went on dry land, house B stood its ground. The foundation stood tall despite all odds.

This idea holds true in our relationships. Once you have built your marriage on love, you can believe without a doubt that when storms come, and they will come, you can rest assured that your relationship will stand tall in the midst of it. The storm symbolizes marital problems such as financial problems, busy schedules, poor communication skills, bad habits, daily stress, sexual problems, inability to have children, disciplining the children, the in-laws interfering and religious problems, just to name a few. No relationship is immune to these types of problems. Marital issues, like the storm, will come from every angle. They will come because that is just the way it was set up on planet earth. Do not question "why" You cannot ask the question "why me." Why not you? Who would you rather have experience these problems? Make a list of names of all the people you would rather have go through these types of marital storms. If you make that list, rest assured that someone you know may have also made their list and written your name on the top of the page. So, you see, there is no running away from these marital issues. They are inevitable. However, if your relationship has a deep foundation in love, then you and your spouse should be able to weather any storm when it comes.

The sand symbolizes superficial ideas of what a man should look like and have before he can walk you down the altar. Some people focus on skin color and nationality such as black, white, Indian, brown, Italian, French, Caribbean, Chinese, Japanese, etc. The next type of sand is called emotions. Some believe that love is a feeling. They could not be further from the truth. They think that if the person makes them smile, laugh, cry, feel happy, ecstatic or have the feeling of goosebumps that they are in love, or the person loves them. If you wake up one day and some of these emotions are not present, does this means that you do not love the person anymore or the person does not love you? Love is not an emotion. It is a principle. You cannot build a marriage on feelings. Feelings are like clouds, you know that they are there yet within seconds they may be gone out of thin air. As human beings, we tend to change with age. This means our emotions are always changing. What made you laugh in the past might not matter to you in the future. Whereas the characteristics of love are never changing. They are always true.

Another type of sand is called the body sand. Here are some examples. Short, tall, slim, slender, plump, heavy-set, short haired, long haired, blond, brunette, gray, bald, blue eyes, black eyes, brown eyes, green eyes, pointy nose, flat nose, dimples, beard, or clean shaven. Another sand is called the career sand. Such as a nurse, lawyer, pastor, medical doctor, pharmacist, stock broker, architect, and six- or seven-figure earners. All of these things are superficial. It does not mean that once a man fits your profile he is the one for you. This is nonsense. If you were to marry a man because he has a certain skin color, a certain hair type and an amazing career where he can fund your lifestyle appetite, what would happen when he loses his job and his hair begins to change due to nature? Would you love him still? Of course not. Your reason for marrying him would have been gone. All these things are superficial. This might sound ridiculous, but it is the truth. These things do happen.

This is one of the reasons why the divorce rate is so high in America and in many parts of the world. People are getting married for the wrong reasons. If you were to build your relationship with these types of "sand," then the minute the storm comes, your relationship, or marriage, would be destroyed just like house A. If you build your relationship that eventually will turn into a marriage on a foundation of love, then, yes, when the storm comes, your marriage would be able to weather the storm. As the quote said, "love never fails." Love is the only foundation that can withstand any disaster. This is why there are marriages that last for more than 50 years. So, choose love. Head into a relationship with someone who shows you love. Once you see the foundation of love in a man, then this is your sign to head to the altar. This is the one for you.

Chapter 2

Availability

> "We can't plan life.
> All we have to do is be available for it."
> -Lauryn Hill

A very long time ago there was a woman by the name of Naomi. She was married and gave birth to two sons. The name of her husband was Elimelech. Her two sons were Mahlon and Chilion. Elimelech took his family from Bethlehemjudah to a country called Moab. They went to Moab to escape the famine in Bethlehemjudah. Sadly, Elimelech, Naomi's husband, died and she became a widow. Then, both of her sons died as well. This made her two daughters-in-law also widowers. As a woman in her old age, she had to bury her husband and her children. Most parents would rather their children bury them and not the other way around.

The names of her daughters-in-law were Ruth and Opah, from the country of Moab. After the death of their husbands, Naomi told them that they could leave her and go back to their families because she was going back to her own country. Well, they were tied to Naomi through marriage. The death of their husbands broke the tie. Opah, said her goodbyes and left. However, Ruth decided to stay with Naomi. Naomi allowed Ruth to go back home to her family. Ruth told her no and that she would stay with her. According to the story, Naomi was a wonderful individual. She was loving and kind to others and to her family as well. Ruth saw her as a positive person who could potentially influence her life in the right direction. So, she told Naomi:

Intreat me not to leave thee,
Or to return from following thee,
For whither thou go, I will go
And where thou lodge, I will lodge
Thy people shall be my people
And thy God my God.
Where thou dieth, I will die
And there I will be buried
Ruth chapter 1 vs 16-17

Both Ruth and Naomi journeyed back to Bethlehemjudah. Ruth was a foreigner, and not well-received by the people. She saw a man by the name of Boaz, who, based on the story, was hard-working, attractive and kind. She became interested in him. She told Naomi that she will choose his field to gather grains. Even though there were other fields in the area, she wanted him to notice her. This was why she made that decision. With certainty, it worked like a charm. Naomi encouraged Ruth and gave her her blessings.

Boaz did take notice of her. Actually, he noticed everything about her and what she was going through. He noticed that people were mistreating her because of her nationality. He noticed that all though her husband died, she was willing to stay with her mother-in-law to help her out. He saw that the grain she was gathering was not just for her, but rather for herself and Naomi. He went to her and told her that she should only gather grains from his field. He made it known to her that no one in his field would bother her or mistreat her.

At times, he would give her grain and provisions to take home. One day he invited her for dinner. She ate at his table and they both broke bread together. According to Ruth, she was overjoyed. She told Naomi how happy he made her feel. She explained the joy that she received when talking to him. Then Naomi told her to do the ultimate act.

Naomi told her that she should go to his house and after he has finished eating and drinking, she should cover herself and walk to where he is sleeping and lay at his feet. Wow, reading this, you are probably thinking, "how desperate is Ruth in finding a man?" Ruth knew what she wanted. She knew that he was a good man. Boaz treated people with kindness and compassion. Also, she believed in her mother-in-law and that she would not lead her in the wrong direction. So, she obeyed and did exactly what Naomi told her to do.

Since she was so interested in Boaz, Naomi told her to let her interest be known to him. It was ok to smile at him, to talk with him and to become overwhelmed with joy when she would see him. All of that meant nothing if he did not notice or realize that she really wanted him for her husband rather than a friend. Naomi told her to lie at his feet.

Boaz finally awakened from his sleep and saw a woman laying by his feet. Ruth was covered so that no one would see her. When Boaz awoke, he was startled. Then Ruth showed her face to him and he was happy it was her.

He did not take advantage of her. He told her that he cared for her and that she was the type of woman that he wanted in his life. So, he told her that he was going to meet with the leaders of the city as quickly as possible so he could marry her. He then asked her to cover her face and go home so no one would see and recognize who she was. Shortly thereafter, they were happily married.

There are a few key points of this story that I would like to highlight. The first key point is that Ruth made herself known and available to Boaz by gathering wheat in his field on a consistent basis. Therefore, because of her constant presence in his field, Boaz was able to take note of her. Based on the story, Ruth noticed Boaz before he noticed her. I hear many times, of ladies who want to get married and live happily ever after but find it difficult to meet the right guy, but how do they make themselves available?

According to research and centuries of studies, we learned that the lion is the king of the jungle. Lions kill and eat almost every animal in the animal kingdom. I saw an episode on National Geographic, where a lion actually pursued an alligator into the water. Alligators have their full strength in the water, yet, the lion pursued it and almost killed it. Lions have no fear. They know what they want, they know who they are, and they know that they are feared. However, you will rarely see lions attacking the herd. For example, when lions see a herd of gazelles, they lay and wait until one of the gazelles is by itself then they make their attack. This kind of attack gives the lion more of a guaranteed success to their kill.

The gazelle straying away from its pack, is a sign that it is available to be hunted and served as an entrée for the lions which are lying in wait. The same goes for women. Sometimes you have to make yourself available by straying from your group of friends so that a man who is interested in pursuing you can begin his pursuit. I am not saying that you cannot hang out with your girlfriends. What I am saying, however, is that you should once in a while stay by yourself and give yourself a chance of being noticed.

The next time you are on a lunch break from school or work, go and eat by yourself. When you go to church, tell your friends that you will talk to them after church and go sit alone. Once in a while you can take yourself out to dinner and a movie. All this might sound a bit ridiculous and crazy. Let me explain why doing this makes sense. You are with your girlfriends and you see a guy who is checking you out. For some reason, he is brave enough to walk up to you and your friends and singles you out. Now what is the most possible outcome? Some of your friends might think that you are more beautiful than they are. Maybe some could get a bit jealous but would be happy for you.

The worst thing I believe could happen is you falling for the guy but become discouraged because of your friends. For example, some of your friends might say that he is too tall. Others might say that he is not tall enough. A few of them could say that he is short. While one may say that he is not handsome enough. They might criticize his facial hair or the lack thereof. Some could just come out and say that they do not like him or that he is ugly. All of this negative energy could discourage you to the point that you then agree with them. I am not saying that your friends are wrong to voice their opinions. Everyone has different taste. For this reason, your friends would definitely tell you how they really felt, although doing so could come off as them being negative. In addition, some of your friends may actually do their very best to be negative. That is just how life is.

Now on the other hand, what if you met that same guy when you were alone. The guy walks up to you and introduces himself and then you do the same. A two-minute talk could lead to a three-hour conversation. That conversation leads to a date. Then the date leads to happiness in your life. At that point, you tell your girlfriend about the guy you have met and how amazing he is. Your friends are so happy for you and cannot wait to meet him. Then you finally let him meet your friends. Your friends begin to compliment him in front of you. They compliment his height and weight. They talk about how handsome he is. They tell you how much they like how he keeps his facial hair. They are so happy for you that he makes you happy and they are automatically happy.

Ask yourself this question. Why would your friends potentially say negative things to discourage you from going on a date with the guy, yet encourage you to stay with him after you have fallen for him? The answer is that we, as humans, are quick to say and see negative things first. We are quicker to discourage than to encourage. We are quicker to say you cannot than to say you can. This is how most people are by nature. This is why it is better to start a project before you tell your friends and family what it is that you are doing. It is best to get to know someone enough before you introduce them to your loved ones.

There was a chef who wanted to open up his own restaurant in one of the busiest areas in New York City and he told his friends. They told him that the competition was too high. They told him that he was going to waste his money. Then they told him that it would not make sense to try because it would be too expensive. Then finally, he rented a space to open his restaurant in the same city at the same busy location. He needed help, so he asked those same friends to help him paint and move his furniture into the restaurant. They were happy to help him and get his place ready for business. They then told him how successful he was going to become. He was complimented on the type of chef that he is and that his customers were going to enjoy his cooking.

All of a sudden, his friends became motivators. We have to understand that it's not all of the time that our friends are trying to be negative. I do believe that sometimes our friends basically want the best for us. They do not want to see us fail. They do not want us to feel embarrassed by not reaching our goals. So, this is why they sometimes would tell us that we cannot do the thing we want to do just to prevent us from tasting the bitterness of disappointment.

Ruth understood this from the beginning. To guarantee success, sometimes we have to stay clear from our friends and families. Sometimes we have to do things alone and not share our goals and dreams with others until we are finished or actively working towards our goals. The very act of going after our goals and what we want can be the thing that can help others to think positively. Ruth could have stayed with the women in her area and have lady talks but no, she wanted a husband. She heard of Boaz and she wanted him. Like the gazelle, she strayed, she put herself in a position so that Boaz, like the lion in the jungle, could roar at her.

After Boaz and Ruth were married, they had a boy. The name of the boy was Obed. When Obed became a man, he had a son and called him Jesse. Jesse then had a son and called him David. This David was the little shepherd boy who killed the giant Goliath. He placed a stone in his slingshot and aimed it directly towards Goliath. Goliath fell down and died. This is the same David who became King. King David had a son and called him Solomon who was the wisest man to ever live on planet Earth. Whenever you know what you want, and you make yourself available to receive it, good things will always come through for you. Use the story of Ruth to help you.

When Ruth moved to Bethlehemjudah with her mother-in-law, Naomi, she became the breadwinner for the house. Naomi was in her old age and could not perform rigorous labor. Ruth took it upon herself to go to the field and reap wheat for herself and for Naomi. According to the story she was a very hard worker. One day she was working, and Boaz asked to have dinner with her. She gladly said yes. She quickly went home and told Naomi the good news. She wanted to zero in on every opportunity possible to be with Boaz. So, she was ok with taking a few hours away or even a day off work to have dinner with him.

    I am deeply saddened at the sight of beautiful single women studying and working themselves to death yet going to bed alone. They never have the time to go on a date because they are always studying. They never have the time to hang-out after work because they are always working. They are always doing something important. They are always occupied. As I said in the earlier chapter, there is nothing wrong with making money. However, one must be careful because the constant working for money can interfere with what is most important. What is most important is the ability to love and to be loved by someone.

    In the United States and many other countries, employees are given sick days, vacation days, holidays and personal time off from work every single year. The number of days varies from country to country and from job to job. Also, since we may accumulate personal and holiday time, we should use that time up before we lose it.

This means that if you come across someone who cares about you and treats you like the queen that you are, you should do something about it by making yourself available to spend time with that individual. It would not hurt if you were to call out sick so he can treat you to a dinner and a movie. One sick day should not make you lose your job.

You acquire sick time, so why not use it. If he wants to take you away on a four-day cruise to get to know you better you should go. Tell your director or supervisor that you want to use some of your vacation time. Saying yes to a man sometimes does not mean that you are easy. It sometimes means that you are as interested in him as he is interested in you. I am not saying that you should do this all of the time. Once in a while you can do it. Just make sure he possesses the characteristics of love. Besides, how would you know if he possesses the characteristics of love if you constantly drown yourself in work, school and other activities all the time? You have to make yourself available to meet and spend time with Mr. Right.

The second key point is Ruth listened and took advice from someone who had a happy marriage. That someone was Naomi, her mother-in-law. We have to be careful who counsels us and gives us advice. The fact that Ruth left her place of birth to go with Naomi meant that she really respected her. There are individuals in this world, such as our sisters, our brothers, our mothers, our fathers, our neighbors, our friends and our coworkers, who might not want the best for us. This is very disturbing. There are people who want to see you do well, but not better than them. Some people want to see you happy but not happier than they are. Others want you to be sad so you can be sad with them. These are the individuals you must steer clear of if you want a more meaningful life.

The sad part about this is that most times these individuals are the ones whom you love. Ruth loved her mother-in-law. So, when she told her that Boaz asked her to have dinner with him, Naomi gladly encouraged her to go and spend time with him. She wanted the best for her. Naomi had an amazing marriage, so she wanted Ruth to have what she had. I have witnessed what is called male bashing many times. Male bashing is when a group of women gather around to say negative things about men. They talk about their dislikes and why they hate men. They talk about all the bad things that men have ever done to them. They discuss how men need to know how to talk to independent women who have great careers. They talk about how lazy some men are. They talk about how abusive men can be at times. They go as far as to say that they'd rather stay single than to get back in a relationship in fear of getting hurt again.

I believe it is ok to have a discussion about issues such as these. Sometimes you have to get certain things off your chest and clear your mind. This is why discussion groups can be equally referred to as group therapy. There is a problem, however, with women who are a part of the male bashing committee who are themselves happily married. Who, while attending the male bashing group talk and actively saying negative things about men, are texting their loving husbands with kisses, hearts and smiley face emoji's. I am talking about married women who go home to their loving husbands. These women I am talking about, are women who thank God every day for giving them good husbands who love them and treats each of them like a queen. They are so happy to go home on a cold night knowing that their husbands are home ready and waiting to put their arms around them and make them warm. Then eventually, one thing leads to another. The holding then leads to touching, which leads to kissing. The aggressive kissing then leads to caressing every area of the body. The heavy breathing then creates a non-understandable sound of passion which only the individuals involved could comprehend.

Unfortunately, these happily married women are agreeing with their fellow ladies that men are animals and that it is impossible today to find a loving loyal husband. This is wrong on every level. All they have to do is say it is true and that some men tend to mistreat women. There are good men out there like their own husbands. If they could find love, you can find love, too. Unfortunately, this is not what is being said at the male bashing group meetings.

Mother Teresa once said, "I will never attend an anti-war rally; if you have a peace rally, invite me." It would make sense to say that an anti-war rally and a peace rally mean the same. Do they really mean the same thing? The word anti-war is against war, which is true. Here is the big problem. The word anti-war has the word war in it. What do you think of when you hear the word war? When I think of the word war, based on history, I think of death, crime, murder, losses, funerals, widows, fatherless children, motherless children, overcrowded hospitals, amputations of human limbs, fear, pain and suffering, just to name a few.

On the contrary, the word peace means something totally different. When you think of peace, you think of happiness, laughter, freedom, family and friends, loved ones, tranquility, joy, tears of joy, and a clear mind, again just to name a few. This is why we have to be careful of what we say and the words we use. Words are powerful. They mean more than we think they mean. This was why Mother Teresa refused to attend an anti-war rally. She did not want to have the thoughts and emotions of what the word war means. However, attending a peace rally would give her the positive emotions and feelings that the word peace stands for.

So, with this understanding, the male bashing group should be dismissed and a new group that is called male uplifting should be assembled. In this group, rather than saying what you do not want, you say what you want. For example, do not say that you don't want a man to cheat on you. Rather, say that you want a man to be faithful to you and you alone. Say that you want a man to respect you and treat you like the queen that you are, and not that you don't want a man to yell at you and treat you like you are filth. This exercise can be a bit difficult. However, with practice anything is possible to rid yourself of negative behavior, especially when you've had your heart broken.

I understand where most ladies are coming from. It is true that men at times, including myself, have done so much hurt to women in the past. We men are sometimes the reason why a lot of women are angry and bitter. We at times take women for granted too often. Sometimes we raise our voices too much. We tend to not follow through on our promises. We pursue other relationships while we are already with someone. We lie to other women and tell them that we are single yet we are engaged or even married with children. To add insult to injury, some men look at a woman with disgust when she gains a few pounds after having given birth to their own children. This is wrong on every count. Men from the year one to year 2017, have made many mistakes. I believe, without a doubt, that men will make mistakes in the years to come as well.

    I myself have made many mistakes in the past. I knew that I was not ready for a serious relationship, yet I lied and toyed with the hearts and minds of many women. I did not have the characteristics of love a few years ago. This meant that I was very quick to anger. I did not have control of my anger so I, sadly, at times, would yell and speak in an aggressive manner towards the ladies whom I was seeing. I did not have a conscience at that time.

    I remember a long time ago, I promised to take a young lady out for dinner. She was excited, and she told me yes. So, I planned the date for us. The plan was to take her to dinner and a movie in New York City. At the time, I was addicted to the pool hall. Most times after school my friends and I would take a trip to the pool hall and play all night. I started to see an improvement in my skills so I began playing for money. Sometimes I would win and sometimes I would lose. Winning money was never the reason for me to play the game. Just playing the game alone was enough to satisfy my passion. I loved music at the time, I still do today, however playing pool actually took over my life and became my obsession.

The day that I told the young lady that I would take her out on a date was the same day I had planned to compete against someone at the pool hall. I figured that I could play a quick game then leave in time for my date. Well, that was the plan. The day finally arrived. I heard the school bell ring signaling that school was over for the day. I then packed up my belongings and gathered my friends so we could head to the pool hall. When I went outside I was in shock! Apparently, it was snowing all day. The snow was halfway to my knees. The temperature was close to zero. I was not discouraged by the weather. I made up my mind that I would make my way to the pool hall no matter how bad the weather was.

After 35 minutes of toiling in that ridiculous weather, I was finally able to walk into a warm heated building filled with loud music and laughter. My table was ready for me. My competitor was already there warming up and getting ready to take my money. I then played a few rounds of pool with my friends to get myself ready to walk away with $100. Time went on and after a few rounds with my friend, we decided to start the competition. I was the one to break. I went for my stick and I picked up the chalk and chalked the tip and placed it in between my pointer finger and my thumb on my left hand.

Every few minutes my phone would ring. I just refused to answer it. About two hours after, I checked my phone and it was the young lady who was calling me the entire time. She was outside in the cold at the train station waiting for me. I called her back and told her that I was going to leave in a few minutes. My few minutes became a few hours. I left the pool hall after 10pm that night. I was supposed to meet with her around 4pm. The sad part about this story is that I was thinking about how I lost the game and forgot I had a date. I remembered I did the young lady wrong the day after. I was young and foolish at the time. She was hurt and told me that she cried. The entire day I was not man enough to call her and say I was sorry. I was on my way to school when I saw her on the train. She confronted me and forgave me way before I said I was sorry.

Yes, I made mistakes in the past. Am I still that person? The answer is "no." The man I am today would look at the man I was in the past with disgust and shame. Human beings can change. The last time I checked, men are also human beings. This is why the male bashing group has to be dismantled. A guy who hurt you in the past can change and be a man of honor and loyalty to another lady after he has realized that he needs to change and become a better man, like myself. So yes, you were hurt in the past, but you can still be optimistic of the future. The future is always brighter and full of hope. If you dwell on the past you will never be able to move on. You have to be able to move forward and must leave the past in the past and make yourself available in order to find the man of your dreams.

The third key point is Ruth took a chance. She could have gotten rejected; however, she took a chance anyway. Sometimes we have to take a chance and put ourselves out there especially when we know exactly what we want. Ruth knew that Boaz was the man of her dreams so she did exactly what her mother-in-law told her to do. She laid at his feet while he was sleeping with hopes that he would accept her. I believe that she thought about all the possible outcomes. Outcome number one, he could have accepted her and told her how much he loved her and that he wanted her to be his wife.

Outcome number two, he could have rejected her and said that he only liked her as a friend. That he was just being kind to her because she was kind to Naomi after she became a widow and lost her sons. This was why he protected her and allowed her to gather wheat from his land. These are both legitimate results. If she did not make the decision to try, then she would not have known the answer.

In the year 1935 an Austrian physicist by the name of Erwin Schrodinger performed an experiment wherein he locked a cat in a box with a vile of poisonous gas that could release at any time. Once that box was closed however, no one would know whether the poisonous gas was released so there were two valid conclusions. Conclusion A, the cat would be dead and conclusion B, the cat would be still alive. It is only after he opens the box that a valid conclusion would stand. We have to, and must, put ourselves out there to find love. What if we get rejected? We should never fear failure. Bruce Lee once said, "don't fear failure, but low aim, is the crime. In great attempts, it is glorious even to fail." You see, it is ok to get rejected when you put yourself out there. The fact that you were rejected means that you actually did something. If you tried and succeeded, then it is also proof that you tried. To live a life wondering what could have been if you had just tried is pathetic. Erwin Schrodinger is telling us, based on his experiment, that in life there will always be at least two valid outcomes once we do nothing. However, once we make a decision to take action on what it is that we want, then we would see only one valid result.

What Ruth did to let Boaz know that she loved him was centuries ago. I am not saying that women should do what she did. What I am saying however, is that when you find the man for whom you are looking, and that he possesses the characteristics of love, that you should give him hints that you are interested. Playing hard to get at this moment would be detrimental to your success at finding love. So, take off from work if you must so you may spend time with him. Go out of your way to bring him lunch at his workplace. Pick up the phone when he calls and stop thinking that if you pick up right away he would think that he has you wrapped around his little finger. When he texts you, you should reply when you see the message rather than delay just to be difficult. If he asks to take you out and you really do not have the time, rather than telling him you cannot go out with him, you should ask him for an alternate date. This would make him know that indeed you do want to spend time with him but that you just have a lot going on at the moment.

The sexiest sight for a man is seeing a woman that he cares about showing signs that she cares about him as well. Do not think that you are doing too much, or you are trying too hard. Like the Schrodinger's cat experiment, you will never know the valid conclusion until you open the box. You will never know whether or not the guy you are interested in wants you to be his wife someday or if he sees you as just one more lady friend. Your way of opening the box is putting yourself out there. If he rejects you, then that is ok. If he accepts you, then great. You will never know until you try.

Babe Ruth, one of the most successful baseball players to ever play the game once said, "never let the fear of striking out get in your way." Babe Ruth made headlines for the amount of home runs he made in a single season. However, he also made headlines for the most strikeouts in a single season. He did not fear striking out. His goal was to bat the ball out of the stadium every time. So, if you are rejected by a man whom you thought liked you, all you have to do is keep batting. Once you continue to make yourself available, love will then fall right into your lap.

Chapter 3
Fear

> "The oldest and strongest emotion of mankind is fear, and the oldest and strongest kind of fear is fear of the unknown."
> -H. P. Lovecraft

Without hesitation the General shouted "Fire!" and then there was silence. Les Brown, an amazing storyteller told a story about a man caught behind enemy lines. He was a great soldier. He was very skilled in battle but not skilled enough to avoid getting captured. Once captured, he was placed under arrest and taken to a holding cell. The next morning the General summoned him to the courtyard. He was then taken out of his cell and was dragged by his hands to the center of the courtyard. With his hands and feet in chains, he looked around the courtyard and saw hundreds of enemy soldiers with their weapons drawn and pointed directly in his direction.

His body began to tremble. The temperature was scorching hot, 115° Fahrenheit, yet he was shivering as though it were the day after a brutal snow storm. Tears started flowing from his eyes and his knees were jiggling so much that he lost his balance and fell to the ground. The General walked up to him and told him that since he was a prisoner of war, he would face his death by firing a squad the next morning. Death by firing squad, also known as fusillading, is a type of capital punishment commonly used by the military during times of war. This is when an enemy, or a prisoner, is tied to a pole or a stone. Sometimes they are seated or placed on their knees and soldiers aim their weapon at them and shoot them to death.

The prisoner was placed back onto his feet at the General's order. One of the officers clearly showed him exactly where he would be tied up and where the soldiers would stand to execute him. These soldiers were highly trained marksmen. They were the best of the best when it came to shooting long range and short distances because they hardly ever miss their targets. The prisoner saw the marksmen cleaning and polishing their rifles in preparation for his execution. The General saw pain and fear in the prisoner's eyes so he decided to offer him a way out. The

General gave him a choice. A chance to change his destiny. A choice only he could make for himself.

Before the prisoner was taken to his cell, the general gave him a second option. He told his prisoner that he could choose to walk through the gates of the camp or choose to face his certain execution. The prisoner's emotions went from depression, to despondency, to downheartedness, to feeling crestfallen, and eventually turned to joy and happiness. He suddenly began to smile with the hopes of freedom. Without any hesitation, he asked "what is behind the gates?" The General shook his head from left to right and said, "I cannot tell you, but it is unknown horrors."

Finally, he was taken to his cell for the last time. While in his cell imagine what must have been going through his head. He was probably thinking of the worst-case scenario. I believe he was asking himself questions such as, "what if there is a tank on the other side waiting for the gates to open, intending to blow me to pieces." Or maybe he might think, "what if there were wild animals such as lions, tigers or worse, an anaconda lying in wait to attack me." Based on the story, the prisoner was more terrified of walking through the gates than being tied to a wall and having trained marksmen shoot him to death.

Jim Rohn, an amazing author and a prolific speaker, was talking about how negative people think. He gave an example about a man looking out the window at a sunset. Before the man looked at the beautiful sunset, he looked at the speck on the window. Why is it that humans find it easier to see the negatives than the positives in life? Why did the man focus on the speck on the window rather than on the beautiful view? I am always puzzled by this question. On one hand, the prisoner knew for certain that he was going to die by a firing squad. He knew that his fate was sealed. Yet, a choice was given to him to walk out of the gates and he was terrified of making the decision to walk through the gates.

I believe that it was fear that held him back from making the decision. Fear can paralyze you. Fear is, as one author puts it, "false evidence appearing real." Fear is almost always negative. A lot of what we fear never comes true, yet we hold that fear in our hearts not knowing that the same fear could destroy us in the near future. Another author describes fear as, "forget everything and run." There are two things fear can do to us. One, it can paralyze us by making us stay put where we are and with what we have. Second, fear can liberate us. It can give us the power to feel the fear and do what we have to do anyway. Sadly, we have to be the ones to choose what fears will govern our lives and it was now time for the prisoner of war to make a decision.

Finally, it was day break, and once again he was taken from his cell to see the General for the last time. Again, the question was asked. It was time to make a decision. The General asked him, "do you want to face your fate by firing squad or do you want to walk out the gates?" The prisoner trembled, and slowly mustered the words "what is beyond the gates?" The General only said, "it is time to make a decision." With fear, the prisoner chose his fate. He chose what he knew. He chose what he could understand. The prisoner believed that the unknown might be worse, so he chose what seemed safe. He was then tied to a stone and the sharp-shooters went in position to await the General's order. The General lifted his right hand and yelled, "FIRE!"

After the shots rang out, someone walked up to the General and asked him what was behind the gates. He replied, "freedom." Freedom was on the other side of the gate. Yet, the prisoner chose death by firing squad. The prisoner could not think of anything better than his fate because of his deep-seated fears. Fear had crippled him. He allowed fear to show him only the worst possible outcome. So, he stayed with what he knew, and his life was over in seconds. The Bible says that "the thief comes to kill, steal and to destroy." These are the same characteristics of fear. It comes to steal your joy, your life, your happiness and your potential freedom. The prisoner allowed fear to overtake his mind, then allowed his fear to steal his hopes and dreams of a possible future and eventually it literally killed him.

This idea of fear holds true with relationships. It hurts my heart when I see a lady going through a very difficult stretch in a relationship, a relationship infested with pain and misery, where there is an abundance of infidelity, physical and/or emotional abuse and/or lack of love. This type of relationship should have already been over and dealt with long ago. Yet the lady stays and projects the illusion that she is happy. I have seen many ladies fall into despair because of this kind of toxic relationship. Here is the million-dollar question, "Why would a lady stay in such a situation where she is treated poorly?" Here is the answer. It is because she does not believe that she would be able to find someone else. She decides to stay with her spouse and stays with him in fear that if she leaves him no other man would want her. This is where fear, false evidence appearing as real definition, takes hold of her and paralyzes her causing her to stay in her abusive situation. This is true if her husband is the bread-winner in the home and her income is not sufficient to move out into a place of her own. She begins to doubt herself and rather than going through the gates of uncertainty, which is to walk away from the relationship until it changes, she stays and faces the firing squad. This scenario results in a broken heart and a long life filled with misery.

So, every day she has to ignore the many different perfume scents from different women on his clothing. She pretends to smile when he speaks to her with words that lower her self-esteem. She dulls the pain of a broken nose and lies to her friends and family that the cabinet doors are to be blamed for her injuries. It is difficult for me to grasp that someone would prefer to stay in a situation they are accustomed to, which in this case is something unhealthy and detrimental, rather than to take a chance on themselves.

While writing this chapter, a good friend of mine called me while he was at work. He had a very sorrowful tone. He tried his best to make small talk before he got into the reason for why he telephoned me in the first place. Then finally, he told me what happened, which rendered me speechless. He told me that a female police officer who regularly visited his emergency room with her prisoners, was found dead in her home. She died from a self-inflicted gunshot wound. She had killed herself. When I heard this, my heart fell to the ground.

The officer was having marital problems and going through a divorce. According to my friend, she was a beautiful young lady. She was polite and very kind. No signs of pain were ever shown on her face. Based on the news media, she took her own weapon and put it in her mouth and pulled the trigger. For some reason, no one told her about the gate. No one told her that beyond the gate was freedom. She did not know that happiness and love would have greeted her beyond the gates. She only saw one option. That option was to commit suicide. My heart and my prayers go out to her family.

I went online to read up on this sad story and I saw that people who did not know her were heartbroken by the news. They left comments on the news pages and on social media saying that they are praying for her family. I did not leave a comment. For some reason, I did not know what to say. All I was thinking at the time was why it had to come to this. I asked myself, could this have been prevented? Yes, I said to myself. Yes, this could have been avoided. I believed that she waited far too long to file for a divorce. She stayed in that unhealthy marriage longer than she should have.

Time after time she had to endure the pain and heartache due to her situation. If we were to look at the prisoner of war in the story, you would see that before he was taken back to his cell for the last time, he was asked if he would like to go through the gates. If he had just ignored the fear of what was the worst that could've happened outside the gates and rather embraced the empowering fear, which means to forget everything and run towards the unknown and your goals, he would still be alive today. What caused him to panic was time. He was given time to think about what choice to make. Time made his imagination run wild. He died the minute he started to contemplate that the firing squad would be the better solution. This is why we are told in school that when we are taking an exam, we should not second guess ourselves otherwise we risk changing the correct answers to the wrong answers. Most of time the first answer is the correct one.

Therefore, he used the time to create the idea that whatever was beyond the gates was more dangerous than the firing squad. As time went by, the gates became more and more fearful and scary. This, I believe, is one of the things that happened to the young lady officer, causing her to kill herself. She was so crushed by her pain that she probably thought she was no longer beautiful enough for another man to love her. She was smart, yet, because of the constant belittling from her husband, she thought she was stupid and mentally weak. Finally, she was physically strong but the ongoing mental and physical abuse broke her. I believe that these were some of the reasons why the officer and many other victims take their own lives as a way to escape from their pain. No one in their right mind would just put a gun to their head and pull the trigger.

As human beings, our number one goal in life is to survive. We want to live as long as we can on this planet. We want to live a long, productive life and raise families. When we are sick, we do our very best to fight to go on living. We are willing to cut down on smoking, heavy alcohol consumption and the amount of animal flesh we consume just so we can successfully fight off deadly diseases and add years to our lives. So, when you hear stories like this, you tend to ask yourself questions. The officer saw no other way out. If she had dealt with the situation promptly, she would have had a fighting chance, but she delayed. All those years had given her too much time to think about fixing this problem. Then one day she woke up and saw that the problem had ballooned into what seemed to be a point of no return. She found out how deep she was inside the hole that made her believe there were only two options open to her. One, to stay in the relationship and two, committing suicide. With all the time she had to debate, the best one out of the two, according to her, was suicide.

Ladies, I am making my plea to you right now. If you are with someone that is making you sick by the way they are treating you, please do something about it right now. Do not delay. The longer you delay the worse the situation becomes. This will then paralyze your will power to move on. The delay will destroy you. So, today, if you are reading this and you are not happy with your partner or your spouse, let them know exactly what your issues with the relationship are. If changes do not happen, or do not come quickly enough for you, then it is time for you to exit the relationship. Do not wait until it is too late for you to move on. You might end up like the officer or you may eventually muster the necessary courage and leave but emotionally you could be destroyed by that time. You would be what is called "damaged goods" if you stay too long in that type of relationship. Yes, you would want to love again but it would take you a lot longer to find love in your damaged state. Try to fix your relationship if you can or get out while you still have your sanity.

There are many reasons why some women tend to feel pressured to stay in an unhealthy marriage. These types of pressures come from their families and friends, religion and often-times their community. Religion, I believe, can sometimes misuse the bible to instill fear in the hearts and minds of church goers or use it to control individuals. This is why I believe that the church is partially to be blamed for why so many women stay in an unhappy marriage. I feel that the bible can be used for many reasons. At times, we tend to use the bible to support our own point of view.

For example, as a child growing up in a Christian home, my parents used to quote the Bible to me a lot, so I would respect them and behave. Whenever I would misbehave my mother would say, "Linton, remember what the Bible says, that you should obey your parents in the Lord, so your days may be long on the earth." So, whenever I would disobey my parents, I would feel guilty and fear I might possibly die at an early age. I would just obey her out of fear of my life being cut short if I disobeyed.

When I started to read the bible for myself, I found that the same bible that told me to obey my parents also said "parents provoke not your children to anger, lest they be discouraged." I could not believe this. My mother did not quote that sentence from the bible to me. She only quoted what was beneficial to her, to her only. Did my mother do this willfully? I think her parents did it to her and her grandparents did it to her parents. This became a way of life for many church goers. At times, I was not happy with what was going on in my home, yet I had to ignore it because I felt I must obey my parents no matter what. However, some of the things they were doing were considered wrong according to the same bible that they quoted to me.

I remember when my sister had gotten pregnant out of wedlock with her first child. My mother and her husband felt a sense of shame and embarrassment. They felt like the church and the community was going to look down on them. They both held a position in the church and felt their lives would have to be perfect. The fear of feeling shame was so bad that my mother was plotting with a few ladies at the church to find a way in which my sister could have an accidental abortion.

They talked about giving her a cocktail to drink or a pill to get rid of the pregnancy, so she could lie and say that she fell in the bathroom and lost her child. They were going to go to great lengths to cover up my sister's pregnancy. Let me make this very clear. I do not believe this is how it is or was with every church. I can only speak for what happened at that church I attended. I do believe however, that this happens a lot in the world where families try to make their daughters have abortions to rid potential shame from their lives. In some cases, if the young ladies refuse to comply with their parents, they are kicked out of their homes. This is madness. Rather than showing their loved ones love, they show them fear and resentment.

My sister felt pressured to follow through with the abortion but thankfully, she did not go through with it. Although she did not know what to expect and how she was going to take care of her baby, she faced the fear of the unknown and later gave birth to my mother's first grandchild, whom my mother loved dearly. Sometimes my mother would fight with my sister because she wanted to spend more time with her grandchild. My mother changed her 3pm-11pm shift to 11pm-7am shift at the hospital so that my sister could go to school while my mother took care of the baby in the mornings. My nephew became my mother's pride and joy. Yet, at one point she had been willing to stop my sister from having the baby.

Most of what I could remember was my mother and her friends telling my sister all about the worst-case scenario and nothing positive. She was told things such as that she would not be able to take care of the child herself while holding down a good job. Since the child's father is not in the country, the child would lack a father figure in his life. She was told that she would not be able to finish school and have a successful life. People would judge her and look down on her because she was not married and yet she had decided to have her child out of wedlock.

All this negative talk was instilling fear in my sister. She was petrified. They were trying to scare her so she would abort her child and eventually steal her potential happiness. As I said earlier, the bible states that the thief comes to kill and destroy. Most times the thieves are the people that we know and care about and who we love the most. These thieves come in the form of our parents, our best friends, our spouses, our pastors, etc.

While I was writing this chapter, I came to the conclusion that my sister did not hear anything positive about her situation. My mother was so focused on telling her how difficult it was going to be to take care of her child, that she forgot that the government has a nourishment program for women, called Women Infants and Children Program (WIC). WIC helps women and their children, from the time they are born until the time they reach the age of five. This program gives women with low income food that can help nourish their children and themselves, providing them with milk, cheese, bread, eggs, 100% orange and apple juices, butter, oil and all the essentials that a mother and her newborn through five-years-old would need to stay in good health. My mother was working at the hospital for many years and she knew she would be able to change her shift because she was good friends with the staff nurses. She eventually changed her shift to look after her grandson.

Why didn't my mother think about these options from the beginning? It was because of fear. Fear kept her mind in a negative state. The thought of feeling a sense of shame from her church friends crippled my mother's mind from thinking positively regarding my sister's pregnancy, which prevented her from seeing the positive side. My mother was feeling the pressure from her friends, so she took that pressure and placed it on my sister. Was this ok? All my mother had to do was to embrace my sister's situation and face it head-on with the possibility of something good coming out of it. Like the prisoner of war in the story, due to fear of the unknown, chose death by the firing squad as a safe result. My mother allowed that same fear, stemming this time from her church friends, causing her to think that making her daughter abort her child would have been the safest choice and the only way for her situation to be accepted.

I was a bit bewildered at the fact that my mother and her church friends thought that my sister doing an abortion was less of a sin than having premarital sex and having a child out of wedlock. They wanted her to lie and say that she fell thereby losing her child. Here is the thing. Part of The Ten Commandments states that we should not lie or kill. To cover up my sister's pregnancy, my mother wanted her to kill her child by means of abortion and to lie about it. This happened in 1997.

Now when I look at the case where the officer killed herself, I ask myself questions. Was she being influenced to stay in her marriage? Did she feel pressured to tough it out with her husband despite how he was treating her? Did her family or church friends tell her that she was better off staying with him because they are doing the same thing as well and that this is just the way it is? I know many married couples who go to church and events together and pretend that they are in love and happily married. Yet, when they go home they separate themselves and sleep in different rooms. Or, they would sleep in the same room, but one would sleep on the bed while the other one sleeps on the floor. They are living totally different lives yet they are afraid to file for divorce out of fear that they will be unfairly judged.

What is going on in this world today? How long can someone pretend to be happy and continue to live like this? This takes us to another reason why some ladies stay in an unhealthy marriage. There are some cultures and religions that look at divorce as wrong. At times, divorce is frowned upon and has a negative stigma attached to it. Here is the thing, I have never heard of a married couple that were in sync with each other and so in love that they decided to get a divorce. That would be absurd.

People stay in this type of marriage for fear of going through the divorce process. This process can be daunting and dreadful especially if there are properties and children involved. Still, it is not a valid excuse to stay. You have to remember that your children will grow up and become adults one day. They will get married and move out of your home and leave you alone with your spouse, a spouse who does not love you. Then what? What are you going to do then? Grow old miserably? Or file for a divorce in your old age and die alone hoping to find a man to love you then?

If he is constantly cheating on you, you should leave and file for divorce despite what others might think. When you have mustered the courage to leave him, you will realize that you are saving yourself from a lot of heartache. For example, in today's world, there are a lot of STD's that are out there. The worst of them all is HIV/AIDS. This disease is circulating this world on a rapid scale. Millions of people die of HIV/AIDS every year. If you fear leaving your husband, then you are putting yourself at risk of getting this deadly disease. Is your marriage worth receiving a death sentence? What good would you be to your kids and a possible future spouse, if you were dying? It would be impossible for you to be there to attend your son's soccer practice and your daughter's piano recital if you are always sick and in pain. It would be extremely unlikely that a man would want to marry you, knowing that you had previously contracted a deadly disease.

One of the first things to do is to destroy all of the excuses for why you cannot leave your adulterous abusive spouse and just move on. You have to take the chance of uncertainty and walk through the gates. You must remember that fear breeds excuses. Fear will give you all the reasons why you should stay. It will remind you to think of your children and that your children need to grow up with both parents. It will tell you that your church and your community will not accept you so you are better off staying. Fear would go as far as to make you feel like you would never be good enough to find someone else. Are these statements true? Fear is a liar and the devil! It comes to steal your joy by making you feel like there is no hope so you might as well continue in your pain and suffering.

There is a song written by Flanders and Swann that can explain the damaging effects of excuses:

There's a hole in the bucket, dear Liza
Then fix it dear Henry, dear Henry, dear Henry,
With what should I fix it, dear Liza, dear Liza,
With a straw, dear Henry, dear Henry, dear Henry,
But the straw is too long, dear Liza, dear Liza,
Then cut it dear Henry, dear Henry, dear Henry,
With what shall I cut it, dear Liza, dear Liza,
With an axe, dear Henry, dear Henry, dear Henry
The axe is too dull, dear Liza, too dull.
Then, sharpen it, dear Henry, dear Henry, dear Henry,

With what should I sharpen it, dear Liza, dear Liza,
With a stone, dear Henry, dear Henry, dear Henry,
But the stone is too dry, dear Liza, dear Liza,
Then wet it, dear Henry, dear Henry, dear Henry,
With what should I wet it, dear Liza, dear Liza,
With water, dear Henry, dear Henry, dear Henry,
But how shall I get it? dear Liza, dear Liza,
But how shall I get it? dear Liza, with what?
In the bucket, dear Henry, dear Henry, dear Henry,
In the bucket, dear Henry, dear Henry, in the bucket!
But there's a hole in the bucket, dear Liza, dear Liza.

As you can see from the song, the last sentence takes you back to the beginning. This is what fear does to us. It gives us all of the excuses to not take a chance on ourselves and do the things we have to do. So, we complain, argue and cry about our situations, yet we make no attempt to change our circumstances because we have so many excuses for why we cannot try. By not taking chances we then end up stuck in the mental chains of doubt. This eventually makes you feel like you have to accept your situation by allowing your spouse to treat you in any way that he pleases. Ladies, the minute you were conceived you were special. Do not let anyone tell you differently. You were placed on this earth to love and be loved. You are the light in a man's world. Everything about you is beautiful. You are queens and goddesses. You are to be loved and respected. You have to show your self-worth at the beginning and stay true to your values in your relationships. The minute your spouse hurts you by cheating on you or verbally and physically abusing you, you should put a stop to it right away. Never let the abuser feel that what he did was ok. Let it be known by calling the authorities, separating yourself or even have your spouse see a counselor. Please do something this very instant to avoid it from happening again.

The officer, in the story above, allowed her husband to cheat and abuse her so long that she lost all of her sense of self-worth. She probably believed that no one would ever love her and care for her because she was too broken. The pain of hurt was so severe that she thought no one was able to ease her pain. Her only solution was to do what made sense at the moment, which was to kill herself. She knew that putting a weapon in her mouth would guarantee an end to her suffering. Let me repeat myself. THERE IS HOPE, FREEDOM, HAPPINESS AND LOVE BEYOND THE GATES. Please, you have to believe this statement is true.

Even though you may not believe that there is hope beyond your situation, you have to at least try something. You have to try to ignore the negative voices in your head. Fear is crippling. However, inaction breeds fear. So, does it hurt to try to believe, despite your doubts and fears? John C Maxwell, a very notorious author said that:

> "There was a very cautious man
> Who never laughed or played.
> He never risked, he never tried,
> He never sang or prayed.
> And when he one day passed away,
> His insurance was denied,
> For since he never really lived,
> They claimed he never really died."

Trying is living. My mother has been dead since 2010 and to this day she cannot try anything new. She cannot try to sing a new song or try to lose weight. She was a phenomenal cook yet she cannot try a new recipe because she is dead. As breathing human beings, we cannot be like the cautious man in the quote. He never really lived so he never really died. So, is he a living dead? This is what we become when we do not take chances on ourselves. The prisoner of war in the first story above did not try to walk through the gates for he feared most the unknown, which was behind the gates, more than facing his death by fusillade. I guess we can truly say that he was already dead before he was tied up and shot.

According to her biographer, J.K. Rowling experienced unhappiness in her marriage. Her suicidal thoughts were one of the direct results of her decision to separate from her husband. She believed that she was worth more than what she was experiencing in her marriage so she decided to leave him. She took her child and walked through the gates of uncertainty knowing that she would find hope, happiness and love. Was it easy? No, it was not. J.K. Rowling encountered some difficult times. She was living in a very small apartment with her daughter and at times had to rely on the government to help her because she was without a job and was considered poor. This was another factor as to why she was depressed and thought of killing herself. She could have gone back to her comfort zone, which was the house that was filled with unhappiness and a total lack of love. Instead she decided to tough it out. It was her pain and suffering that pushed her to dedicate herself to her writing.

She stated that, "I was set free, because my greatest fear had already been realized, and I was still alive, and I still had a daughter whom I adored, and I had an old typewriter and a big idea. And so, rock bottom became the solid foundation on which I rebuilt my life." Had she stayed with her husband and continued to be miserable, Harry Potter would have been nonexistent. As we all know, she has become a prominent author after the publication of the first Harry Potter novel; she went on to write an entire series of Harry Potter books which eventually became international best sellers and she sold the film rights, generating a movie franchise which immediately hit the top of the box office charts. She allowed the definition of fear which is to forget everything and run, to push her through the gates. Choosing to walk through the gates of uncertainty was a difficult decision I can well imagine. Yet she made that difficult decision. She took a giant leap of faith. Today, J.K. Rowling is one of the world's most successful, best-loved, widely read and wealthiest authors.

The story about the officer was a little extreme. However, I felt compelled to include it in this chapter to show a worst-case scenario. I have met many bitter women, at my job, on the train, at church, at the mall, you name it. I used to shake my head when I would hear a lady make negative comments towards men justifying their reasons for being single but now I understand. Some of them stayed in an uncomfortable relationship for far too long and the minute they got out of it, who they were as a person was destroyed. They had become damaged goods. They neglected the gate of uncertainty that could have led them to peace and happiness and now that they were finally out, they found themselves lost, or worse, infected with an STD.

Their negative attitude became apparent to other men who had nothing to do with why they are hurting. They wear their pain on their sleeves. Any man whether good or bad, who comes along and tries to get to know them is pushed aside with hate, resentment and fear. This is talked about in chapter eight, which describes some reasons some ladies are single and how they push men away. I personally believe that in life both sexes are part of the problems and part of the solutions. We have the power to change our destinies.

We can change our future and we can create our own happiness. First, we have to value ourselves. We must respect who we are. Sometimes others will treat us a certain way based on how we treat ourselves. Or worse, they will test us to see how far they can push us before we either break or stand up for ourselves. So here is the simple solution, you must value yourselves. In so doing, others will value you as well. Please do not allow the pressure of society, your friends and family or religion to tell you how you should act and what you should do to be happy. I repeat, if there is a problem in your relationship you should get it fixed. If your spouse does not want to change then do yourself a favor and get your things together and leave. Leaving will not only save your life but it could give your spouse a wake-up call and let him know that he has to change, and that he needs to treat you better. If that does not happen, then you will be able to move on with your life. It will be much easier for you to find someone to love and respect you when you, are of sound a mind, a healthy body and disease-free than when you are badly broken, both physically and emotionally. As Jim Rohn always says, "if you are not happy with the way things are going, then change it. You are not a tree."

Chapter 4
Changing

> "If you change the way you look at things,
> the things you look at change."
> -Wayne Dyer

Mr. Speaker, they called him, was well known in his time. He was asked to speak at a major event and did his research on the topic of his message. He practiced and rehearsed his delivery every single day leading up to his speaking engagement. He was known to be a perfectionist. Everything had to be in place before every event and the way in which he rehearsed his delivery had to be the exact same way he would portray his message, otherwise, it was all a failure to him. Normally, he would sit in a dark quiet room and from memory, recite his lines while imagining that he was in front of an audience. Finally, he was ready. The event was at hand. He walked in the building, waved his right hand to the announcer, signaling him that he was ready. The announcer let the audience know that the speaker was present. There was a long round of applause while the speaker was walking onto the stage. Then he began to speak.

While he was delivering his message, he noticed that there were some people talking back and forth to each other. Yet he continued. He knew that his message made sense so he did not allow those individuals to deter him from fulfilling his purpose that day. He then heard folks laughing at what he was saying. Nevertheless, he kept going. At one point, the people that were talking were amplifying their voices with no regard for others who were trying to pay attention. Seeing this, the speaker continued to deliver his message. Shortly after, he saw a group of people walking out of the auditorium. For a few seconds, he began to question himself on whether or not his points were being misinterpreted, because he was so confident in his message even though people were leaving the auditorium. He was puzzled to see people walking out during his speech. However, this did not faze him one bit. So, he continued with certainty that there was someone in the audience actually learning something from his speech.

While he was coming to the end of his speech, he saw at the left of the stage a few individuals fast asleep. Before he began to second guess himself again, right next to the people that were sleeping, he noticed a group of individuals taking notes. He saw that they were taking notes like they were writing their books. Every time he would say something they would put their head down and write. This gave him joy. He smiled, nodded his head up and down, said his conclusion and walked off the stage knowing that he had delivered his message exactly the way he had rehearsed it.

He was well received by the audience. There were cheers, whistles and shouts, followed with a hefty long applause. People were lining up to shake his hand and to take pictures with him. He did not seem to be amazed by the overwhelming display of gratitude because this was something he was used to. He pretended to smile and show a little enthusiasm for his appreciation.

A lady walked up to him and said, "Mr. Speaker, I would like to speak to you." He replied, "sure, how may I help you?" She said, "I loved your message. It was what I needed to hear. I have traveled over 100 miles just to hear you speak and you did not disappoint me." There were a lot of people waiting to speak to him, so he told her to hurry up and get to the point. She went on, "how were you able to continue your presentation with all the distractions coming from the audience?" The speaker asked, "what distractions are you talking about?"

She began to explain, "well, from where I was sitting, I heard a few individuals speaking loud enough for me to hear and I was nowhere close to the front. I am sure that you heard them."

"Additionally, I saw many individuals walking out of the auditorium." The speaker looked in the lady's eyes and said, "is that all?" The lady ended by saying, "you did not feel discouraged when you saw some people sleeping and a few laughing at what you were saying?" "No, not at all" he said. He saw that the lady was confused.

The speaker's eyes were wide open. He continued with a big smile of amazement and said, "I know it was great!" The lady was surprised with the speaker's response. The speaker continued, "the individuals that were talking are called talkers, because talkers talk." She began to nod her head up and down showing that she agreed. The speaker went on, saying, "those who were walking out of the auditorium are called walkers, because walkers walk. The ones who were sleeping are called sleepers, because sleepers sleep. Also, the individuals that were taking notes are called note takers, because note takers take notes."

The speaker knew that his message was properly delivered. However, he did not change his message because of the responses he was seeing from the audience during his speech. He continued with confidence, believing in his ability to speak and deliver his message. I believe with no doubt in my heart, that this is an exact replica of what life really is. In life, we have to stay true to who we are and never change due to outside distractions. Sometimes we tend to change or adjust our personalities and behaviors based on what has been thrown at us in the past. This is what we call human nature, but does this make sense?

I had a long discussion with a young lady who is a very good friend of mine. She was telling me how much she has changed and that she is not the same lady she used to be. She explained, and I felt sorry for her. I actually had pity for her because she was so ignorant of the fact that she was causing her own unhappiness in her life. She did not realize this. Based on what she told me, she was the kind of lady who would go out of her way to please her man and make him happy. Pleasing people was in her DNA. For example, she was dating a guy who would prefer to have a home-cooked meal rather than restaurant food. So, being the person she was, she would do her best to cook for him. She would find the ingredients to make the food taste exactly how his mother would cook it. At times, she would utilize social media like YouTube, to show her exactly how to make the meal identical to how he liked it. She did not feel that this was doing too much. She actually found pleasure in making him happy.

She was also the type of lady who not only took pride in her appearance but also took pride in her man's appearance. For this reason she would go shopping for him. She was not rich, so she would wait for sales, look for deals and coupons, so the little money she had could stretch. She knew what he liked so every now and again she would pick up an article of clothing for him just because she wanted to. There had been a situation that caused him to drop out of college and she knew that he really wanted to finish his degree. Being the kind and loving lady she was, she dipped into her personal savings account to help him get back into school so he could better himself.

She was the type of lady who loved and cared for her guy. Sometimes, she would call her guy her king. Most ladies would have called her crazy for doing so much for him. Yet, she believed that they were in love and that her actions stemmed out of that love. According to her, he treated her like a queen and he made her feel special. She felt special when she was around him. She said she felt safe and loved when he was with her.

Sadly, that relationship did not last because of his infidelities. The lust of the flesh overpowered him. He was weakened by the sight of other beautiful women. The minute he began to cheat on her, everything about him changed. He started to ignore her phone calls and lied that he did not see that she was calling. He had to lie because he was with another woman and did not want the other lady to know that he was in a serious relationship. He stopped appreciating her for who she was and what she was doing for him and for her deep commitment to their relationship. He became a selfish human being only thinking about himself. He took advantage of her. Men like him do not deserve to be in a relationship with a woman like her.

This was a slap in the face for her. She had thought that he was the one. After all, she sacrificed and gave of herself, body and soul; her heart was broken and trampled on. She was devastated to the point of depression. She could not believe that he would have become a guy who was dishonest, a cheater, a liar or a person who would break her heart. There is a quote that reads "I can control what I do and say to you, but I cannot control what you do and say to me." We have to take this quote to heart because it is so true. Our goodness cannot make anyone good. You treating someone with respect does not mean that someone will have respect for you in return. We can only control our own actions. I believe that once we accept this truth and make it dear to our hearts that we would then have no more worries.

    She was very good to him, but she could not control how he treated her. Just like the story above, the speaker delivered a great message, yet some individuals walked out, fell asleep, spoke back and forth to each other, while only a few took notes and were appreciative of his message. Two amazing things happened in that story. One, the speaker continued presenting his message despite the distractions. Two, in the face of the many distractions only one group of people were listening and taking notes. Only a few individuals were actually learning something. That was what he wanted to know. He knew that not everyone would pay attention. The lives of the individuals who did pay attention and valued his message could possibly be changed after absorbing his message. This is why he stayed true to his message and kept speaking.

It pains my heart when I meet and listen to amazing women who are finding it difficult to keep a man. I have seen women cry and get in a state of depression because they cannot keep a man in their lives. Here is the problem: What made them great women was destroyed when they were hurt in their previous relationships. To avoid being hurt again, they changed into someone else. They change into ladies who hardly show love and care towards their man. They changed from someone who used to love cooking to someone cooking once in a while and doing more ordering out. They changed from being women who would always show love and affection to women who are lifeless and affectionless. They changed from women who normally show interest, to women who show no interest whatsoever. So, guess what? No man in his right mind wants a lady like that in his life. They do the next best thing; they run far away from them.

Now let me ask you, the reader, a few questions: What if the speaker had changed his delivery in the middle of his presentation because of negative feedback from the audience, would the change to his delivery automatically make everyone pay attention? Do you think that the individuals who were sleeping would suddenly wake up? Would the talkers then become mute? Would the people who walked out of the auditorium, and probably went in their cars to go elsewhere, somehow turn their cars around and return to hear him speak? Just think about these questions for a few seconds. The speaker did the right thing. He kept on speaking. He did not change his message to suit his audience. He took time to write and to go over his message and he believed it was sufficient for his audience. He stayed true to his prepared message.

You have to continue to be the lady you are. The lady who shows affection and love. The lady who shows compassion and care. The lady who goes out of her way to please her spouse. If you are a lady who loves to cook for your spouse, then cook for your spouse. If you are the lady that trusts your spouse, then trust your spouse. If you are the type of woman who loves to see her spouse dress well and look his best, then go out of your way to help him with his appearance. Do whatever you like to do in a relationship to make your spouse feel appreciated.

I am not saying that these are the things a lady should and must do. No not at all. All I am saying is that if you are a loving lady who loves to do things for her spouse then you should not change who you are because of what happened to you in the past. Do not change who you are because of what you have been through. You have to remain 100% who you are and stay true to yourself, despite your past hurts. You have to keep doing the things that you love. You never know, you might be two bad break-ups from finding your king. You may be two break-ups away from meeting a guy who will honor you and respect you the way you deserve to be treated.

What if you were two break-ups away from coming home to a spouse that is so into you that he makes you a bath with rose petals and silky lavender soap, so once you get in and sit down, you could feel the smoothness of your skin? While you are lying in the tub, he is massaging your feet because he knows you were on your feet all day. With tears in your eyes you would ask the question "why me, why am I so lucky to be loved like this?" Here is the answer, it is because you are an amazing woman. You make your spouse feel special every day. You did not allow your past hurt to change your character. You faithfully remained who you are. You have allowed the past to stay in the past. So yes, it was time for you to find your king and for your king to find his queen.

Remember however, the question I have asked: What if you are only two breaks-ups away from finding your king? You must note that the spouse you are seeking is also out there looking for you. Ladies, we have all had our share of hurts. This is what life is. The sun comes up and it goes down. After winter is spring. After spring is summer. Then right after summer is fall. We cannot complain about the changing seasons because no matter what we do or say, the seasons will continue to change like clockwork. We have to accept them for what they are.

It is the same way with men. Some men will cheat. This is why we call them cheaters. A lot of men will lie, and they are called liars. Others abuse women, so we call them abusers. Then you have men who love and respect their women and treat them with overwhelming love. These men are called lovers. If you allow the hurt and pain you received in your former relationships to change you, then you will never have the perfect spouse. You might possibly meet him but, because you have become a different person, because of what you have gone through, you will never keep him. He will meet you and run as far away from you as possible. You have to shake off the dirt from your past, this is the only way you can move forward.

About four or five years ago, I was in New York City sitting on a bench in Battery Park. I was experiencing a lot of stress. The stress was too heavy for me to carry and had escalated to the point where I found it difficult to leave my house and go to work. I saw that I failed at everything so whenever I would embark on a new project, before I started, I would doubt myself and tell myself that I was going to fail just like I failed in the past.

This was truly a self-fulfilling prophecy. I wanted to reach my goals but because I had failed so many times in the past, I believed that there was no way in which I could succeed this time. My mind was so full of doubt that I gave only about five percent effort towards my goals. I had always been a guy who normally gives 100 percent, all possible effort, but this time I just could not muster the energy to do so. With that said, I did not reach my goals. Again, I failed. Did I fail because the task I was embarking on proved to be too difficult? The answer is no. I failed because of me, because I no longer felt successful.

So, I found myself dressed in a suit and tie sitting on a bench in Battery Park not knowing why or how I had become a failure. I needed to speak to someone, so I telephoned my father. I told him exactly what was going on and he told me not to worry. He told me that the only way I can move forward is by shaking off the dirt of my past failures and run. I did not see where he was going with this. I guessed that he knew that I was a little confused based on the simple fact that I was quiet and not responding to what he has just said.

He then made his point very clear. He told me about a guy who had dug a large hole so he could bury his horse. After digging the hole, he lowered his horse in the hole and began to shovel dirt on top of the horse. The horse was a little unconscious but the constant shoveling of dirt to his body brought him back to a conscious state which gave him energy to stand up on all fours. Though he had no way of escaping because the hole that his master had dug for him was extremely deep. However, he did one action over and over and over again. Every time his master shoveled dirt on his back, he would shake it off. Whenever he would shake off the dirt, the dirt would fall under his feet. Then he would stomp the dirt for as long as he could. He kept doing that action until the hole was filled to the top, which gave him the opportunity to run away.

My father was trying to tell me that dirt, like our past hurt from our experiences, can do one of two things. It can bury us if we allow it to or it can propel us to greatness. In agriculture, the word dirt is called soil. Soil is nourishment for a seed so it can grow. Without soil, the seed would never grow. It would not even have a chance. Therefore, if we were to look at our past failures and heartbreaks as nourishment that is essential to our growth, we would then understand how much of a value our past really has. We would then see things differently. Like the owner of the horse, he saw the dirt as substance to bury the animal and on the other hand, the horse saw the dirt as something most beneficial to his escape.

Having said that, we have to enter every new relationship as if it were our first. We have to show love the way we usually show love. We have to go that extra mile to make our spouses happy if going the extra mile is what we like to do. Yes, as human beings, it can be difficult to forget the past. However, we cannot allow our past to influence us in how we treat our new spouse. The bible explains this perfectly. It says that in order for us to go to heaven, we must be like little children. Understand this, little children have what I call a Temporary Children Alzheimer's Disease. This means that they are so quick to forget that you spanked them. You can spank your child and a few minutes later they come and hug you. Then eventually, within minutes, they go back and do the same thing again.

This is how we have to behave and what we must learn to do when we enter a new relationship. My friend in the story above changed completely because of what she went through. Today, I do not think that she knows who she is. She is lost and confused. She enters every relationship on the defensive. If she calls or texts a guy she is dating and if he does not reply within minutes, she would then text him angry messages and end the relationship because she thinks he is seeing someone else. If her boyfriend has to work late and he reschedules their date, she would go to his job to see if he was actually at work, just to make sure. This is not who she really is as a person. She has become like this because of what happened to her a long time ago. So, whenever she meets a new guy and demonstrates this type of behavior, the guy then feels uncomfortable and moves on to someone else. The end result is that she remains single and complaining that it is hard to find a good man.

I am zeroing in on this message because I want you to know how detrimental it is to change from the person you are to someone else. To conclude this chapter, I want to give you one last example of someone famous who managed to remain true to who he was despite all odds and eventually found success.

Colonel Sanders, at the age of 65, was considered broke as he reached retirement age. He was living in his car and driving around the country to sell his fried chicken recipe for two long years. He went from door to door, restaurant to restaurant with hopes to make a sale. His goal was to sell his recipe to restaurants and make a little commission from each chicken sold. It sounded like a great idea, but the execution was challenging.

He understood the quote from Winston Churchill that reads, "success consists of going from failure to failure without loss of enthusiasm." For Colonel Sanders, that was exactly what he did. He believed in his recipe so much that he stayed true to it despite his failures. He received a lot of rejections until finally he made a sale. This was how the KFC franchise began. As of today, there are 20,000 KFC locations globally in 123 countries. Colonel Sanders stayed true to his recipe and his business plan despite his many setbacks.

Likewise, ladies, you should stay true to being who you are despite what you have experienced in the past. Just keep being the awesome, wonderful woman you are because one day, and pretty soon, someone will come along and be amazed by you. That someone could be only two break-ups away. You never know. Please develop the Temporary Children Alzheimer's Disease, and continue to be the lady you are. Trust me, it is worth it.

Chapter 5
Traditions

> "Tradition is an explanation
> For acting without thinking."
> -Grace McGarvie"

In the dictionary, according to Webster, the word education simply means the action or process of teaching someone, especially in a school, college or a university. Another definition explains education as the act or process of imparting or acquiring general knowledge, developing the powers of reasoning and judgment, and generally of preparing oneself or others intellectually for mature life. Can someone receive an education without attending an institution? Is a diploma the only proof of education? Society on the whole, tends to dictate how we should live our lives and what is accepted behavior.

At times, we tend to follow the teaching and the ideas that are given to us without thinking for ourselves. For example, what we eat, how we dress, how we speak, what to look for in a spouse, what spouse is suitable, what is beautiful, etc. I have learned that many times the guidelines of society are predicated on its culture, geography, nationality and sometimes religion.

I am perplexed at the idea that educated individuals find it difficult to think and reason on their own. So, they take whatever society gives them without questions. Let us just think for a moment. Try to free your mind from science, tradition and the teachings of society for a few minutes. It has been drilled in our heads through schools, universities, media, religion and from our parents that cow's milk is good for our bodies. There have been numerous media campaigns that have hired A-list celebrities to drink milk and leave a milk residue on their upper lips with the catch phrase "Got Milk?" There is also the popular quote which states "Milk does the body good."

Now here is my question, do we need to drink cow's milk in order to have a strong, healthy body? Once again, please free your mind from the traditional way of thinking for now. How about we take a look at the difference with a human baby and a calf, which is a cow's baby. At birth, a human baby weighs on average 7.5 lbs. (3.4 kg) and this number varies depending on whether the child is male or female.

On the other hand, the average calf at birth weighs on average 65 lbs. (29.5 kg). This number is also varied based on the sex of the calf. In nine months, a human baby is still a baby. A nine-month-old baby weighs between 16.7 lbs. to 21.11 lbs. (7.5 kg to 9.5 kg). This child is still dependent on his mother and others for food and survival whereas calves have grown to adulthood by the time they reach the age of nine months. In nine months, a steer bull weighs in at approximately 550 lbs. (250 kg). These bulls can weigh a little less if they are not commercially raised on a factory.

The milk produced by a cow is meant for a cow. The nutrients in a cow's milk are meant to feed its calf so that it can grow and eventually weigh over 550 lbs. (250kg). It is not a coincidence that a calf grows so rapidly. They drink the milk that was made for them. Yet, we as humans drink their milk. The milk produced by a human mother is for her human baby to consume. This milk has nutritional values that can and will help that human child to grow, but not at an alarming rate like that of a cow. This is why the average weight of people living in the United States of America, for example is between 164.7 lbs. (74.7 kg) and 194.7 lbs. (88.3 kg), which places us as one of the fattest countries in the world.

I hope that you have cleared your mind for the moment. Now with that said, do you think we actually need cow's milk in our bodies to grow? I believe that we really do not need it in our system and I became aware of this in my 20's. I was also taking what society told me and blindly following. I would really love to see an experiment where the scientist gives a new born calf milk from a human being and see how fast that calf would grow. I believe that the calf would die of starvation. Although the milk of a human being has nutrients, it would not be of sufficient nutritional value for a cow.

On the flip side, the cow's milk has nutrients which are in excess of the nutritional value a child, or an adult, needs. Just look at the size of cows versus the size of humans. There is a major difference. That difference is weight and size. If you saw a human being weighing over 400 lbs. (over 181.4 kg), you could truly say that person must have an eating disorder. We know that it is not normal for a human to weigh more than 400 lbs. If you saw an adult cow that only weighed 194.7 lbs. (88.3 kg), you would think the cow has fallen on some tough times.

I am not a scientist. All of what I have written here is based upon personal knowledge. However, I did some research and was able to investigate and learn on my own. I used to struggle with my weight which forced me to think outside the box. The box in this case, is the teachings and the guidelines of society. The sad part about these societal guidelines is that we tend to allow them to govern our lives and that anything outside of the proverbial box is seen as wrong and is therefore frowned upon.

I have met so many beautiful, strong, independent, career driven women who complain that it is difficult to find a mate. They were told, based on the guidelines of society that a man with a diploma or a degree is a suitable husband. They were told that an ideal prospect is a man who has achieved a state of financial stability.

They go looking for a possible husband with that idea in their minds. With this mindset, they tend to judge a man before getting to know him. They ignore his good qualities because he does not have proof of an education, and financial success is not manifested in his lifestyle. Thus, they end up choosing the wrong man. This is just insane.

Let us look at a track and field star named Usain Bolt. He is considered the fastest man on planet Earth.

Today he is 30 years old and he has already won 23 gold metals and 5 silver medals. The medals that matter the most are the ones he received at the Olympics. He took part in three back-to-back-to-back Olympics track and field events. The 2008 Beijing Olympics, the 2012 London Olympics and the 2016 Rio de Janeiro Olympics. He took part in 3 events and in each of his three Olympics games. He ran the men's 4-by-100-meter relay, the men's 200 meter and the men's 100 meter. He came in first in all those events. He even did something better than just win medals, he broke Olympic records in most of those events.

    Now imagine Usain Bolt, the fastest man alive, is getting ready for a race. Before the race begins however, he voluntarily ties his feet together with a 30 lb. (13.6 kg) weight. Then he ties a chain around his waist and hooks a 50 lb. (22.6 kg) weight to that chain. Suddenly he hears the announcer through the loud speakers say, "on your mark, get set, go!" When the race begins he then takes off. He begins to run but he finds it difficult to pick up his feet. So, eventually, he comes in last. He complains that he could not move as fast as he had hoped. The world would say how can a man who is faster than the speed of light lose a race so badly? He is in shape. He has won many Olympic gold medals in three different track-and-field events. He is fit and well-trained; how did he lose the race?

Here is that answer. He lost the race because he was tied down with chains. This amplifies my point for women who despite being successful in their own right, they remain single and approaching old age because they are looking for a man who is a degree-holder thinking that this equals financial stability and happiness. This mindset is a heavily weighted chain that is tying them down and keeping them from getting to the finish line, which is finding the ultimate spouse.

In December 2010, five months after my beautiful mother was buried, I attended a stock option event in New York City. The tickets cost me about $1,100. Expensive yes but it was well worth it. Most of the speakers worked on Wall Street and the others had their own financial firms. I learned so much about stock options and how they work and the kind of money you can make investing in the stock market. However, the real eye opener was when I found out that most of these individuals did not have a degree. Yet they worked on wall street and owned successful financial firms. I, at the time, believed that a degree was the only way to have a skill, get a good job or better yet to be respected, but was I wrong.

With my curiosity, I began asking questions. Thankfully my questions were beginning to get answered. Someone at the event asked me, "how did you learn how to ride a bike?" "Did you attend a bike riding University?" "Did you read a book on bike riding?" I was in awe! I did not read any books on riding a bike. I did not attend any institution on bike riding. I learned how to ride a bike by riding a bike. I fell many times, yet I picked myself up and continued until I was able to balance myself.

Then eventually I started to do tricks on the bike. I rode my bike without holding the handles. Later I was able to put a friend on the back of my bike and ride home. Here is what I am saying. These Wall Street investors learned how to trade stocks by trading stocks. They started selling very small amounts and with trial and error, like me riding my bike and falling off but getting back on again, they were able to do successful trading in the stock market.

So, are these men educated? Yes, they are. They learned to trade by trading. They developed techniques on trading from study and practice. They were able to read balance sheets of the companies whose stocks they were trading. They were forced to watch financial news and read business newspapers to keep up-to-date with what is happening in the financial world. This led to their growing vocabulary and strong work ethics. The things they had learned on their own, through on-the-job training, is actually the same thing business school teachers impart to their students. However, the students have proof of an education, which is called a degree and the self-educated investor can only show his success as proof that he is educated in his field.

I normally talk to a lot of women about the qualities they are searching for in a potential husband, and I ask them why they want a man with a degree. The answers vary. A large majority of these women would like to be able to talk to their spouse about politics, social issues, business-related news, geographic-related topics. Some ladies believe that having a man with a degree would not only entitle them to the possibilities of a healthy financial future but would also allow them to fit in with their peers. The social pressure to fit in as an adult is daunting at times. So rather than going after love, they go after what feels right and what is the acceptable norm: a man with a college degree.

Again, try and free your mind from the traditional way of thinking for a few minutes while you answer these questions. Do you think that a man would love you more or less based on his income, the type of degree he has or his lack thereof? Can you date a man who lacks a college degree but who gives evidence of having received an education? Is love based on income, degree or status? Are you seeking a man for love and happiness to start a family or are you seeking status and financial freedom? These are simple questions you can think about when you actually free your mind from the traditional way of thinking.

Look at one of the differences between a man and a woman. A man could see a lady working at a fast food restaurant and based on their interactions, he would ask her out on a date. After getting to know her, he falls in love with her and then he marries her. Whether or not a lady has an amazing income or degree, once a man sees what he likes in a woman he immediately wants her to be his wife. A man's love for a woman has nothing to do with her career path but it has to do with the woman herself. Based on how she treats him and how comfortable he feels when he is with her, is most times the deciding factor on how far he will take their relationship.

Whereas with some women, especially if they have received their education from a university coupled with an amazing career, they tend to at times try to find a man on their level or higher. If he is not on their level in terms of education and income, then she has to look elsewhere. If you are reading this chapter and you notice that this chapter relates to you, please answer this question honestly. What are you looking for in a man? If your answer has to do with external things such as income and degrees, just to name a few, then also answer the next question. Why are these things so important to you? How have your wants and needs been working out for you? Lastly, based on your answers, do you find yourself seeking men for financial security and status or you find yourself looking for a man with a heart full of love who will treat you with care and love you unconditionally?

I have recently reconnected with an old friend whom I had not seen for many years. She was, I thought, exactly the type of lady I was looking for. She was very beautiful. Her smile, her voice and her laugh could always take my breath away. She was what I called the one lady that got away. The minute we reconnected, my excitement went through the roof. We went out for dinner in New York City one day and we began to talk a bit. Most of what was spoken at the beginning was about our past and the things we did together.

In the beginning, everything seemed to go well. Then her true colors began to show. From the looks of it, I could tell that she was brainwashed by the teaching of society. I knew something was wrong. Not that I was judging her and trying to see the bad in her, but I was talking to God in my head saying, "there is no way that I could find the perfect lady so quickly." Everything was too perfect. I was also thinking about finding out her ring size so I could either visit Jared's or Tiffany's and buy her an engagement ring. All of this was going through my head in the beginning of our little talk until all hell broke loose.

Based on the laws of attraction, according to Brian Tracy, "you are a living magnet. What you attract into your life is in harmony with your dominant thoughts." Simply put, what you focus on you will receive. That was indeed true. I was thinking there was no way she could be this amazing. As humans, we often develop negative behaviors after we have been through many tough times in our lives. There you have it; my negative mind was not disappointed. She began to ask me a series of questions. "Why did you not complete your degree?" "Are you going back to school?" "Don't you know that school is important?" She went on and on.

I just sat there and listened. She associated a college education with having a better life, a financially adequate life. She was interested in me but was hesitant to pursue a relationship because I did not have an institutionalized education. With that understanding, her assumptions were that I could never be the type of provider she wanted to call her husband.

She could not see past the fact that I did not have a degree. For me this was a good thing. I knew what she was looking for at the beginning. I know my worth and I will not pretend to be someone else just so I can find love. I will not accomplish a task, like getting a degree solely so that I might be accepted. I want someone to love me for who I am today and not what I can or will become tomorrow. However, I was sad for her. I believe that with the type of mentality she possessed, it would be very difficult for her or anyone in her situation to find true love. She is not simply looking for a husband. She is looking specifically for someone to fit her profile of what she believes will provide her with the love and happiness she craves and feels she deserves. She is a beautiful, well-educated, professional lady who is the victim of tradition and false beliefs. Rather than looking for someone who will love you, care for you and honor you, as humans we tend to look for people with a paper with their name on it. The name would follow the name of the institution they attended for four to twelve years with the potential of becoming financially successful. I am dedicating this chapter to women, not every woman, but to those women who think like my friend.

That same friend of mine today is single because she broke up with the one guy who treated her like a queen. I asked her, "was he a great guy?" She replied, "this was the only guy who actually showed me what true love really means." She broke up with him because he was taking his time to finish his master's degree. While pursuing his higher education, he had many failed start-up businesses, which she actually tried to help make successful. She went on to explain that her frustration with him actually pushed her to mistreat him by speaking to him in a demeaning manner. Yet, according to her, he forgave her and stilled stuck around.

Today, that guy is now engaged to be married. When my friend heard the news, she was very angry that he was going to marry someone else and that he had not asked her to marry him. I was confused for a second. She told me that she did not want him anymore for the reasons explained in the previous paragraphs. She went as far as to say that she was no longer sexually attracted to him anymore just because she was emotionally and physically withdrawn from him. I had to tell her the exact reason why the man did what he did. I told her that he proposed to the lady who loved him for who he was and not for what he was attempting to become in the future or for what she wants him to be.

His fiancée saw an amazing man versus what that man currently has or what he is going to become. She saw a man who made her smile and made her happy to be alive. She did not care about the traditional way of thinking. She saw value in him, so she gave her heart to him and in return he gave his heart to her. Her main objective was to marry a good man who would love her and treat her right rather than marrying a man because of his profession and income. To top it all off, she saw a truly Christian man who loved God and was doing his best to be the man that God wants him to be. This was enough for her to tell him yes. This was good enough for his fiancée but not enough for my dear friend. As she lovingly said, "I don't want to settle."

What does it mean to settle for someone? We are all on the road to somewhere. Sometimes we reach our goals and dreams before others. This is ok. It is what we call life. We should accept others before they have embarked on their journey, while they are on their journey and after they have completed their journey. We all have to start somewhere. The fact that you possess a degree from a university means that you first had to apply to college.

Then you had to complete each semester, one at a time. Then finally graduate. As you can see, it is all about the process.

Here is my question to you. Is it fair for me to judge you because you are in school and still have no degree? Should I look at you differently because you have a degree but have yet to land that perfect job with a great income? Of course not. You have to change the old way of thinking. The traditional way of thinking should be considered out dated. So, when my friend said that she did not want to settle for the guy she was dating because he was taking too long to finish his degree, it made me look at her a little differently. Understand this, when someone uses the word settling to describe a relationship, that person is actually saying that he or she is superior to the other individual. When you say that you are settling for someone, it really means that you think that you are better than that person. It is a way to portray that you are above the person and that person is beneath you. Please understand this, we are all created equal.

Sadly, my friend did not get the message, because right after she broke up with that amazing guy, she dated a professional. This professional man had both a bachelor's and a master's degree. He was her ideal guy. This time, she was dating a banker. According to her, he was successful in his pursuit of higher education and he was positioned for financial success. I felt so sorry for her. She was not happy with the new guy she was seeing, yet she stayed with him. He did not treat her like the queen she is. She did not feel loved in the relationship. She complained and yet did nothing about the relationship. I guess it was ok that he was, according to the teachings of society, an ideal prospect. Let's face it, he was well-educated and had great earnings potential. I guess that's what seemed most important to my friend. Sadly, the relationship did not last.

I did some research and what I found was shocking. According to www.moneynews.com, the average income for registered nurses in the United States is $69,790 per year. That is a great annual salary considering the average annual income in the United States is approximately $50,000 per year. When I had hair, I used to go to my barber shop in Brooklyn, New York. His shop was wonderfully decorated and gave off a comfortable feel. My barber was always into the latest cars.

One day, while he was cutting my hair, I asked him about his new car. Around this time, I was attending a community college. He smiled when I told him that I was going to school. He told me that I needed to have my own business if I wanted to earn an amazing income. I was taken back by this statement. In my head, I was asking myself "how much money is he making cutting hair?" Considering the fact that each haircut was roughly $13 at the time, plus a $2 or $5 tip. I again asked myself, "how many customers can one barber see in a single day?"

Then he gave me the detailed information that led me to understand that barbers can make a substantial amount of income. There are barbers that understand business and the art of leveraging. For example, a barber can use his income from his first shop as capital to open his second shop. In his first shop, he rents his five chairs to fellow barbers and he charges each one of them $400, which is the average monthly rate charged for a booth, locally. He then saves his money and eventually opens a third shop. In all of his shops, he rents his chairs. Now let us do the math.

3 shops with 5 chairs in each = 15 chairs in total
15 chairs x $400 per month = $6,000 per month
$6,000 per month x 12 = $72,000

This income does not include the products he sells in his shops such as sneakers, oil, shaving tools, hats and tickets amongst other things. $72,000 is just his base income. These figures do not take into account his expenses incurred in running his various locations, such as rental costs, utility bills, etc. My barber's shop was right in the heart of Brooklyn, New York, where foot traffic consistently kept him and his chair-renting barbers very busy. He was generating an astounding amount of income, yet he does not have a business degree. What he has is a passion as well as a great deal of ambition. This passion drove him to create his own very successful life. Success did not happen overnight for him. It took time, patience and dedication. Yet he stayed true to his goals and his goals stayed true to him.

I am not stating the fact that having a degree is pointless. To many, having a certificate from an institution can open doors that would not have been opened to them were it not for that document. My goal for this chapter is to educate women that it is pointless to allow society and traditions to make you determine the value of men based on the type of documents they have or the lack thereof. Also, it does not mean that a man with no degree would not be able to provide for his family.

Men are like dogs at times. I am not talking about the dog that walks around and has sex with every female dog and then runs away. However, I am talking about a dog that can sense fear. The minute a dog senses fear in you, he then can attack you. Like dogs, men can sense when a woman is only interested in them because of the kind of degree they possess and the type of money they make. When a man senses this, he tends to use the same thing that draws you to him as a tool to take you to his bedroom and use you for sex, amongst other things then go on his merry way.

I had to say that because it is entirely true. These men are not justified by their actions. However, men have feelings just like women do. A man looks forward to having a wife the same way a woman looks forward to having a husband. If we are interested in a lady and we determine that she is only talking to us because of what we have and what we can offer them, we tend to feel used. We see their love and attention as fake and conditional. A man would then lose all respect for that lady.

We show this by the way we speak to them and treat them. Have you ever seen a man yelling at a lady like she was an animal? Did you ever notice a man cheating on his lady and showing no remorse? These men know that their lady will not leave them because of what they have to offer. They believe that their status, degree and income is sufficient to keep their ladies, so they can continue doing what they are doing with no regrets. What happens most times in this type of relationship is that the woman, through hurt and pain, finally instigates the energy within herself to walk away from an abusive, toxic relationship with the mindset that men are cruel and heartless cheaters.

With this kind of mindset, they blame men for their own pain and problems without realizing that they played a major role in contributing to their failed relationships. This is one of the reasons why there are many women in this world who are extremely beautiful and successful, and yet they find it difficult to find love and happiness. It is difficult for them because they are looking for the wrong traits. It is good to have high expectations, however, your high expectation should have nothing to do with a man's income, status in life or level of education. Your expectations should be about how he is as a person.

Find out his background. Meet his parents and friends. Take a step back and watch how he treats his loved ones. Pay attention to how he treats you. See whether or not he seems to be a trustworthy man. If you are a spiritual, God-loving person, see if he loves and believes in God as you do. Everything else is just on the surface. Your objective is to find that particular someone who will love you and care for you through sickness and in health, till death do you part.

To sum up, do not allow society's guidelines to dictate to you how you live your life. Things will either be wrong, or they will be right, that is a given in this life. Killing is wrong, lying is wrong, stealing is wrong. Yes, those things are wrong. We have to follow the laws of the land. You can choose your own happiness. Ladies, if you see a man who makes you happy and makes you feel alive, then go after him. Don't allow society to tell you not to talk to a man because he does not have a degree, which means that he is not educated, or his income is not sufficient to call you his bride. Your goal is to marry for love and not for money. Please go after love and not after what you can get out of a relationship, because in the end you will complain about how unhappy you are with your spouse. You will finally walk away from that relationship bitterly and say that it is difficult to find a good man.

Chapter 6
Speak Up

> "It took me quite a long time
> To develop a voice,
> And now that I have it,
> I am not going to be silent."
> -Madeleine K. Albright

As a little boy growing up in Jamaica, I was a big fan of karate movies. I would watch them as often as possible. I loved karate movies so much that I would watch them every day of the week. In my neighborhood most weekends, my neighbors would put up a giant projector screen at a dead-end street. We called it Sunday Matinee. My favorite fighters were and still are Jackie Chan, Jet Li and Bruce Lee. I am a fan of the old school fighters as well. Their names are not popular, but they can sure kick some ass!

I started to practice karate moves on my own without any formal training. I noticed that my skills were actually improving. Well, I was never black belt-worthy but compared to my friends, I was a ninja. No one could have defeated me in a fight. I used to do a lot of cartwheels with and without putting my hands on the floor. Back flips were my favorite. Many times, I would climb a fence or a tree and jump off backwards without using my hands. Then one day tragedy happened.

I remembered it like it was yesterday. One morning I woke up and it was pouring rain outside. The rain came down from morning till about four in the afternoon. This was the time I got home from school. I went inside the house and changed my clothes. Then of course, I went outside with my friends and we talked about karate movies. We were sitting on a tall fence. The height of it was about nine feet tall. While we were talking and laughing, we started to imitate some of the karate moves that we taught ourselves from watching the television.

I, for some reason, stood on the fence and flipped backwards without using my hands. What a big mistake. I have done that flip on many occasions and it went well. However, this time something went wrong. There was grass in front of the fence and I forgot that it rained earlier which, if I had taken the time to think, I would have remembered that the grass was still wet from the rain.

So, this time I jumped, but rather than landing on my feet, I landed on my back. I slid across the wet grass and eventually landed right on top of a big stone, right on my lower back. The pain was so severe. It felt dreadful and was unbearable. However, it did not stop there. After I got on my feet, which took me a few minutes to stand up, I found that I could not turn my head from left to right. The pain was so fierce that if I tried to turn my head in any direction, the intensity of the pain would increase.

I went home and struggled to take a shower and tried to get some rest hoping the pain would go away because getting rest could cure me from a potential back injury. Well, was I wrong. My father came home and he called me to come to the table. I went around the table to eat and I tried to ignore the pain. I tried my best to move my head as little as possible. Sitting on the chair was making the pain even worse because I had to keep my back straight which was also putting pressure on my spine. I do not recall what I was eating that day but I do remember that the simple act of chewing and swallowing what I was eating was very unpleasant.

It did not take my father a long time to notice that something was different about me. I was the only boy, and still am the only boy amongst my sisters. As the only boy in the house, I was the most energetic person. It did not matter where I was, at church, in the living room of my house, in my room, in the kitchen or even at the dinner table. I would run around the house, sometimes while we were eating, and I would bother my sisters and try and take their food. Occasionally they would just give it to me so I would leave them alone.

As a kid growing up, I had a very serious stuttering problem. Sometimes it would be very difficult for me to speak. Yet I was always the loudest kid in my home. Although it would take me a long time to say a word, I did not care because I was going to get it out. Especially when I was around my family, I did not feel embarrassed of my speech problem. I would talk so much that my sisters would complain to my father and ask him to tell me to be quiet. This was why my father was a bit curious about my behavior. He was not used to seeing his son quiet and still at the table.

My father eventually asked me if I was ok. I told him that I was doing fine and that I was just a bit tired. I was lying through my teeth. No one knew that I was rendered speechless because of the severity of the pain in my back. I was hurting yet I lied to my father and told him that I was alright. Eventually I left the table and went to my room. I started to cry. Yet, I tried to keep quiet so my father would not hear me. He really cared about my well-being. I thought he would have been angry at the fact that I jumped off of a fence and landed on my back. I did not stop to think he would care that I was hurting.

In just a few minutes after I left the table to go into my room, my father walked in and sat on my bed. He'd come in to talk to me. He just loved talking to his son. He took one look at me and saw the condition of my face and how I was toiling just to look at him. He then asked, "what is wrong with you?" I told him and right away he called for an ambulance. The ambulance crew placed me on a stretcher and when we arrived at the hospital they put me into a wheelchair.

I was hurting, yet I did not tell my father what was wrong with me. He is not a mind reader. I should have told him earlier. Sadly, I delayed. The doctor said if I had waited any longer, that it could have been worse. I could have been paralyzed. Just like that I could have gone from an active kid running around to a kid permanently wheeling himself in a wheelchair.

In my past relationships and with discussions I have had with many women, I have found that sometimes ladies are hurting yet they expect that their spouse should automatically know what it is that is bothering them or what they are in need of. Please make note that men are not mind readers.

A young lady by the name of Lisa, an ambitious independent woman, said that one day she came home from work and her husband made her very angry. She stated that she worked her hardest that day and all she wanted was to go home, take a shower, eat and relax with her spouse. That did not happen because after she got home, her husband was getting ready to leave the house to hang out with the guys. Lisa became very angry at him and he had no idea what was making her upset. He asked, "what is wrong?" "Are you angry because of work?" She said no to every question. He then kissed her and went on his way. Lisa did not tell him that she wanted him to stay home so they could cuddle and relax together. According to Lisa, he should have just known that she wanted to spend the evening with him.

Well apparently he did not get the memo. We men are not built that way. We at times tend to react to situations. We like to please our women. Sometimes we need them to tell us what it is that they want. If my wife walks in the house and tells me how stressful her day was and that she just wants to spend time with me by relaxing together, watching television, and grabbing a bite to eat, I would cancel my plans and spend the night with her. It is that simple. All Lisa had to do was tell her man what she wanted, and she would have received it. Yet, she argued with him, which eventually made him upset. So, he went out with his friends and delayed going home hoping she would be asleep by the time he got in just to avoid any further conflicts.

Here is the problem. Something so small can turn into something humongous. Like me, all I had to do was to tell my father that I fell on my back as soon as he came home. No, I delayed and that could have placed me in a wheelchair permanently. Thank God my injury did not escalate to further damage.

Lisa did not tell her spouse what she wanted and as a result days went by and they both were angry with each other. He was not talking to her and she was not talking to him. Lisa looked at me and said, "he should have known that I worked hard that day and that I wanted to spend the rest of the day alone with him." I asked her how would he have known that? She was speechless for a minute, then she said, "because he should have just known."

There is a text in the bible that states, "we have not for we ask not." Another text says, and this one we are all familiar with, "ask and you shall receive." Ladies, if something is bothering you please tell us. If we are doing something you do not like, please inform us. If you want us to give you something or do something for you then please let us know. You have to speak up ladies. I do not understand how it is so easy for a lady to complain and argue about the things that men do that they do not like and yet wind up speechless when it comes to telling a man what they really want. It all comes down to expressing what you actually want and need. The entire world knows that women are smarter than men when it comes to relationships. This means you could give us hints on what is wrong with you or what you want from us and we still at times will be clueless.

I spent about three to five months in the hospital. If I had gone another day or two without telling my father about my injury, I would have been sitting in a wheelchair for the rest of my life. With that said, if you hold your tongue and not tell your spouse what it is that you want, then that could possibly lead you to getting angry at him.

This can turn into an argument and then escalate to the point where you guys keep distance from each other. Furthermore, it could eventually go on a downward spiral to separation, break up, or worse, a divorce. If you want something good you have to work hard to get it. Also, if you have that same desire to keep what you have then you have to work twice as hard to keep it. That hard work is not really hard at all, it is fairly easy. All you have to do is to open your mouth and speak up.

    When you are angry, you then say things you may not really mean and most likely will later regret. You then use unkind words toward each other that leads to resentment. All this can be avoided if you just ask or say what you want. Do not push your spouse away and then complain that it is difficult to find love. You will be like many other women saying that it is difficult to find love. Really, it's not that at all. Maybe you find it difficult to say the simple things which can eventually keep love in your life.

    Food for thought, "all men are not created equal." We men were created different in many ways. For example, we are different in how we speak, our taste in food, our taste in women, our different backgrounds, our different cultures, our different pasts and different likes and dislikes. Some men are more sensitive while some are less aggressive by nature. I can keep going but I believe that my point is well delivered. The point I am trying to make is that you cannot assume that a man must know to do something or not to do something. Based on his background, he could think that he is doing his absolute best to please you, yet he would become a little frustrated when he gets a negative reaction from his lady.

Tell him to forgive you.

Let me use myself as an example. I am a Christian man who is trying to do my best to follow God as closely as possible. I do my very best to do what the Bible says. Though I may not be perfect, I see myself as a work in progress. There is a text in the Bible that I have been hearing since I was a child growing up and to this day has resounded in me. The text states, husbands love your wives like Christ loves the church.

The Bible is not talking about a church building. Christ does not love a building. He was not nailed to the cross for a building. He died for people. When the Bible talks of church, it is talking about human beings. It is families that makes up the church. This is where the term, "church body" came from. So, based on the Bible, Jesus showed love through His actions for mankind. One way in which Christ showed love was through His forgiveness. He is very forgiving. He forgives, and He forgets.

Once you admit your sins to God, He then is faithfully ready to forgive you. So, if you have made a mistake and hurt your husband and if you see that he is not forgiving you, you should tell him how sorry you are and that he needs to forgive you like Christ forgives us. Show him in the Bible where it says that. There is a good chance that he does not know that he needs to forgive you or to forgive and let it go. Your showing him could be beneficial for him and you.

I was talking to my friend this week and he told me some of the problems he was facing with his wife. I asked him a simple question. I asked, "if your wife were to cheat on you, would you forgive her and continue loving her?" He paused for a moment and said "yes." He said it would be difficult, however, he would have to because that is a requirement from God. He used these words because he knows the Bible. He went on to say, which was an eye opener to me, that, "him forgiving his wife has nothing to do with her but it has everything to do with God." What he is saying is that he honors God by the way he treats his wife. Those words I find to be very powerful.

To stay on topic, my friend has a background in religion. His parents taught him the Bible from when he was a baby. When he thinks, he thinks based on what the Bible says rather than what society teaches. If you find yourself with a spouse whom you love and that you know loves you, but, you see that he finds it difficult to forgive you, you should explain the meaning of forgiveness to him. Maybe it's because of his background. Or maybe he does not believe in the Bible like my friend and I do. This could be the perfect opportunity to explain the Lord's forgiveness to him.

If you already have the understanding and the experience with forgiving someone, then if you love your spouse and want to keep your marriage, you need to teach the art of forgiveness to him. After you have explained to him how to forgive and he still continues to treat you unjustly, then you can easily move on knowing that you have tried your very best. This is not grounds for divorce however, you can then see a marriage counselor and take it from there. You have to make him be aware that you feel distant from him because he has not forgiven you. You have to try to explain to him how sorry you are for whatever it is that you have done and that you feel uncomfortable with the way he is treating you. Do not just sit back and think that it will go away and that everything would go back to normal. Tell him how you really feel.

On February 14, 2017, Valentine's Day, I was at work when I saw a nurse that works in my unit, walking in my direction with a single rose and a big heart shaped balloon. I began to smile but before I was able to tell her that I was happy for her, she came closer and I saw her face. Oh no, it was not a happy sight. She looked confused and a little awkward walking with her present. She did not look like a lady that was happy to receive a Valentine's Day rose and heart shaped balloon. Well, knowing the person I am I said it anyway. The minute she came closer I said with a smile, "nice, I am happy for you." She looked at me and said "what is the point of this? I don't like this."

I then turned, dropped my head down and then turned it to the right with a confused look on my face and asked, "then why didn't you tell him that you don't like these types of gifts, especially when you are at work?" She said, "I don't know, I also didn't want to hurt his feelings." This poor guy actually went out of his way and bought his lady a gift for Valentine's Day. He traveled to her job to hand deliver it to her thinking that she was going to be blown away by his amazing effort to please her and to make her happy. She told me that when he came, she hugged him, took her gift and told him that she had to get back to work. The guy probably drove home with the mindset that she is happy, and she is overwhelmed with joy and probably telling her friends what an amazing man he is.

No, she was not happy at all. Based on what she told me, she is not that type of lady that goes crazy for things like this. Yet, she did not tell him. All she had to do was to tell him the things she likes especially on Valentine's Day. Of course, taking your lady out for dinner is always a win win. However, if you are not into roses then say something. Tell him while you guys are getting to know each other. We have to be a hundred percent truthful with our partners in order to have a happy relationship. We should not pretend or lie just to make our partners feel good. We both have to feel good. If you do not like roses then say that you do not like roses. This would probably make your spouse get you another type of flower, a heart-shaped box of chocolates or a nice perfume. The giver must feel happy to give and the receiver should feel happy to receive. This might sound trivial but think about it for a second. The fact that my coworker showed signs that she was happy about her Valentine's Day gift, I am most certain that her partner will give her the same gift next year.

If not the exact combination, a combination with one of the two.

I was dating someone a couple of years ago and the first Valentine's Day she gave me a gift with a fancy card. She wrote how much she cared and how happy she was to have me in her life. Years went on, and like clockwork she gave me a card every year. She was always excited to shop around to find the perfect card for me. Annually, when she handed me the card I could see how happy she was. I would then read the card aloud in front of her while showing an expression of excitement on my face.

Here was the problem. I do not like cards. I never liked cards. I do not see the sense in receiving a card with words of care and of love written in it with a fancy pen and glitter. It does nothing for me. I did not throw the cards out because I figured I would hurt her feelings if I had done that. I am the type of guy that would appreciate my lady telling me how much she cares about me with words coming out of her mouth rather than off of a greeting card, no matter how nice, no matter how pretty the card is. Putting those words in a card that looks beautiful is just nonsensical to me. I am not a sentimental guy. I was wrong to her. I should have told her after the first card or after the second card that I would rather have a plate of food. I should have spoken up but I did not. She was happy to give me a gift while I was pretending and annoyed to receive the cards she always gave me.

Would it have been so wrong for me to tell her that I do not like cards? Maybe at the beginning. However, she would have understood and got me something else next time, something that I would have enjoyed. The same goes with my coworker. All she had to do was be honest with her boyfriend so he could have an idea on how to please her for certain occasions such as Valentine's Day. Now she is in for a treat because every Valentine's Day that they spend together, he will continue to give her roses and heart shaped balloons until she tells him to stop. So, you see, you have to voice how you feel at all times. Telling your spouse how you feel is crucial to the longevity of your relationship. You have to and must speak up. If you find that your spouse is not forgiving you, you should sit him down and tell him. Or else, since you are a human being, you are subjected to making mistakes in the future and he is going to continue to hold it against you, which is a recipe for disaster.

Tell him how you want him to talk to you.

In the mid 1990s, my grandfather died in Jamaica. He was my mother's father. As a family, we packed our bags and headed to Jamaica. The plan was to stay for a week or at the most for two weeks. After the funeral, my sisters and I stayed with our father since we have not seen him for a long time. My mother decided to leave us with our father for six to eight months and went back to the United States. I was in my early teens at the time and I was just willing to explore my country.

I met some guys around my area and they introduced me to marijuana. They would at times offer it to me and I would tell them no thanks. As the saying goes "birds of a feather flock together." Eventually, I started to smoke a few bags of marijuana a day. I went from smoking once in a while to every other day and finally to everyday. I remember using all the money I had to buy enough for my friends and me. After I was done smoking for the day, I would go home hungry and angry.

For some people, when they smoke too much they become happy and tell jokes. Some would just go to sleep. With me however, smoking brought out the worst in me. Whenever I was high on marijuana, I would go home to my sisters and yell at them demanding that they make me something to eat. I would use foul language towards them. Sometimes, they would hide from me out of fear of me hurting them physically.

I was not aware of this until they told my father. One day my father came home and saw me watching the television and he called my sisters into the living room. They came in front of me and told my father exactly what I was doing and how I was treating them. One of my sisters looked at me with tears in her eyes and said that she was afraid of me because of the kind of tone I was using towards her and that she would sometimes hide from me whenever I would come home high.

I was in total shock. I love my sisters. I loved all of them equally, loved them exactly the same. It hurt me knowing that I was the only guy in the house when my father was at work and rather than protecting my sisters, I was the one they needed protection from. While I sat and listened to them telling my father how awful his son was, I felt so ashamed of myself. The worst part about it was that my father did not yell or get angry. He just looked at me and said that he was disappointed with me. I, Linton C. Samuels, had sisters who loved me and took care of me. I was spoiled as a child. Anything I wanted I had. My sisters loved me, and they still do to this day, yet I showed them my appreciation by verbally abusing them with my abusive language.

Seeing how I scared my sisters with the way I spoke to them, I decided to stay away from marijuana since I was not able to control myself when I smoked it. Remembering what my sisters told me that night, I still to this day do my best to speak to women with love and respect at all times. I have learned my lesson the hard way by hurting the ones I loved the most. This is why I become very slow to anger when a lady disrespects me. I tend to control myself, and make my point like the gentleman that I am.

I speak to women today with respect because of what I have learned from my past. There are many guys who have had a different past than I had. They probably grew up in a home where their father verbally abused their mother and sisters. They may also have yelled and screamed at each other which was not a sign of disrespect or hate but it was just a way of life for them.

A lady with a totally different background would hate to be with a man like this. Let us not be quick to judge. A guy with this type of character is not necessarily the wrong guy for you. He may be the guy that could love you and take care of you the best way he knows how. However, he may not be aware that the way he is speaking to you is wrong and downright disrespectful. He would only know if you told him. You cannot walk away and cry because you feel disrespected. I have never seen tears win battles. Don't ignore it and think that eventually things would change. Ignoring is a deadly disease and does not cure anything. You have to treat the disease with the cure to get rid of it. Same goes with relationship issues.

If your man speaks to you in a demeaning manner, you should, when he has calmed down, tell him how he truly made you feel. Let him know that it is not how you were raised. Tell him that you were raised as a lady and that you have to be respected. Make sure you drive home the point that if he cannot speak to you with love and respect, that you are going to have to separate yourself from this verbally abusive relationship. Remember, it is possible that he does not know that he is pushing you away from him. If he loves you, he would examine your words and respect the fact that you love him enough to share your feelings with him and though you are hurt by him, that you still would love to continue the relationship.

As humans, we are quick to point fingers and judge each other. I was told as a child that I should not eat pork. Therefore, growing up in my home, my parents never cooked pork. Later, I found that the Bible speaks against eating pork. For certain, I stayed away from it; it was not because of what my parents taught me but rather what the Bible said. When I started high school in Brooklyn, New York, I had to wake up at six in the morning to catch the train for school. I would always meet my friends at the local breakfast restaurant, which was very near to my school.

My main breakfast was two eggs and four slices of bacon. I was eating bacon and eggs for three years and did not realize that bacon was pork. A friend of my called me a hypocrite because I always said I did not eat pork yet he knew I had been indulging in pork for more than three years. I was dumbfounded by the fact that I had been eating pork this entire time. The minute I was aware I decided to never eat bacon again. Since then I have never knowingly put bacon in my mouth.

The same goes for men who speak to their ladies with rude tones. It is possible that if you let your spouse know he is wrong for talking to you a certain way, that he could change in an instant. Sometimes you may have to be patient with him and remind him of his tone of voice. Remember, this could be deeply rooted or just on the surface. If he loves you he would put in the efforts to make you happy and change the way in which he speaks to you. Just do not be quick to run away.

No man is perfect. We all need some adjustments. There is always a missing screw we need to make us 100%. Maybe you have the missing screw that we need. Maybe you can fix us. Something so simple as telling your man that he needs to change how he speaks to you can turn your relationship from spiraling downward to shooting up like rockets going into space. So please do not sit by quietly. Become vocal in your relationship and let your spouse know how to speak to you.

Tell him how you want him to touch you.

In society today, we tend to live in what I call a microwaveable time. Everything has to be fast paced and ready at the snap of our fingers. We no longer have the patience to wait. Especially countries with busy cities such as France, Spain, Great Britain, The United States of America, Canada and some parts of China, just to name a few. We are always on the run. Families used to cook breakfast, lunch, and dinner but because they do not have the time to break an egg and put it on a hot skillet, or put some rice in boiling water, they head to the fast food restaurants for most of their meals.

In the United States, fast food restaurants utilize the drive-thru mechanism. These fast food restaurants are sometimes open 24-hours a day. Seeing the vast amount of success that fast food restaurants have been receiving, other businesses now utilize this same technique to maximize profits and customer service. Today, rather than waiting in a bank to deposit your check or withdraw money from your account, you can now drive your car into the drive-thru at your local bank and avoid standing in line for a long period of time.

To go to the extreme, some states have drive-thru weddings. Yes, that is right! That is not a typo. You can drive your car in the drive-thru and a licensed individual of the state would open the window, stick his or her head out the same way they do it at the fast food restaurant, and legally marry you. It only takes a few minutes and you would be legally married in the United States. Once the person is finished deliberating, the couple can say their vows, sign their papers and then go on their way so another couple behind them can drive up to the window and get married as well.

With this fast-paced world that we live in, we tend to allow it to spill over in our relationships. We do not take the time to allow our spouse to understand us and know how to please us. We just assume that they should know right away how to touch us and to make us feel loved, safe, cared for or satisfied sexually. If we are not satisfied, then we can just move on to another person and start another relationship. Just like the fast food drive-thru. If you were to go to a McDonald's drive-thru and you are not satisfied with their customer service or they ran out of what you want, then it is ok, you can just drive to Wendy's or Burger King.

The thing with fast food restaurants is that most or all of their meals are pre-cooked. All of the food needs is to be submerged into some oil for a few minutes or placed in the microwave. Then it'll be ready in five minutes. There is a science behind fast food that is not talked about. Have you noticed that their foods make you happy when you eat it? Once you bite into that burger and dip your French fries in the ketchup, you instantly feel alive. The reason why you feel like this is because of the food. The food consists of three major ingredients. These ingredients are salt, fat and sugar. These ingredients have been tested and it has been proven that human beings love this type of composition in their food, hence the reason why many people are addicted to fast foods.

Also, marketers know exactly how to advertise their products to keep their customers coming back to their restaurants. Have you ever noticed that 99.9 percent of all fast food chains consist of only three major colors? These colors are red, yellow and green. For example, KFC and Wendy's are both red. McDonald's colors are red with yellow golden arches. Burger King's colors are red and yellow with a slight blue. Starbucks color is green. Applebee's is green and red. Fridays and Ruby Tuesdays are both red with black writing, the list goes on.

Did you ever take the time to wonder why these colors are used so often? There is a reason. Of course, we use these same colors for traffic lights and traffic signals. Red means stop, do not enter and wrong way. Yellow means slow down. Green means go and direction. This idea is used in holiday and event themes. For example, Christmas colors are mostly red and green. For St. Patrick's Day, the color green is used. For Valentine's Day, the colors used are red, pink and black, but red is the dominant color.

Marketers and scientists have been studying the taste buds of human beings for decades, which is why their methods are so effective. With that said, a man meeting you for the first time will have no idea on how you want to be touched. He would try to figure it out on his own which could take some time. We do not have centuries to study women. This is why you have to be patient with us. Every woman is different and the only way a man can totally understand how to properly touch his lady sexually is if she tells him with her own words or shows him or does something that will let him know both what to do and how to do it. Don't just up, get angry and leave because the lack of patience can cause you a lifetime of loneliness or unhappiness.

Again, allow your spouse to take his time to understand you. Give him some hints every now and again. Once in a while, speak up and let him know that you want more affection or less affection. I am not just talking about sexual activities among husband and wife, however, once in a while voicing your wants, needs and dislikes in the bedroom could not hurt, but more so in general. I read a quote that says, "greatness takes time, it takes 13 hours to build a Toyota but six months to build a Rolls Royce." Here is my question for you, do you want a Toyota relationship or a Rolls Royce relationship?

The reason why it takes so long to build the Rolls Royce is because the Rolls Royce is mostly hand-crafted. Almost everything is done by hand. So, if a worker makes a mistake on a car, then the mistake would only be on that one car. They are very detail-oriented. Whereas the Toyota goes through an assembly line like that of the fast food restaurant, and in a few hours you can take it for a test drive. How often do you hear of a mass-produced product recall for an expensive luxury item, such as a Rolls Royce? Toyota had a recall for over 5.8 million vehicles in January, 2010. This was just one of many recalls that this company had to endure.

I am not saying that Toyota does not make great cars. I am comparing, however, the vast difference between Toyota and one of the most expensive cars in the world. Look at the difference in price for both cars. One of the cheapest Toyotas is valued at $15,250. This model is called Yaris. The most popular Toyota is called a Camry with a starting price of $23,070. On the other hand, let us take a good look at one of the world's most luxurious cars, the Rolls Royce. The Rolls Royce Ghost entry level model has a price tag of $250,000 making it very difficult for the average person to afford, especially with the average personal income under $50,000 a year. One of the most common Rolls Royce is called the Phantom, with a hefty price tag starting at $417,825 and climbing upwards of $1.2 million. Sometimes customers customize their Rolls

Royce by saying specifically what they want the interior and the exterior to look like.

Based on the customer's request, the price of the car would increase. However, the time to make the car would remain about the same. So, you can see that it is best to take your time with your spouse. Just tell him how to touch you every now and again. It is going to take time ladies. Sooner or later, he is going to know and understand your body in and out and then use your body like an instrument. In time, he is going to be able to, with a few touches, make you smile and sing on the top of your lungs. You will be able to reach high notes you never thought you could reach. Now, here is my question to you, "do you want a Toyota relationship, or you want a Rolls Royce relationship?"

Time equals value.

I believe that a Rolls Royce relationship is a lot better than a Toyota relationship. If you find a man who tickles your fancy, and he adores you and makes you feel like a queen, please do not try to skip any steps. Please do not get annoyed because he does not speak to you the way he should, or he does not touch you the way you want to be touched. Give it some time. Just allow the relationship to grow on its own. However, you should voice how you feel if you are not comfortable or not happy with certain things. This is the only way he would ever possibly know.

I am stressing this topic because I really want women to know that men think differently than they do and we will never think like women do. A man once told me the he was upstairs in his room with his wife and there were about 15 children on the first floor. One of the children was his little girl. While he was talking to his wife, he heard the children yelling and screaming at the top of their lungs. The adults that were with them could not get them to stop yelling. Well, it was a birthday party so what they were doing was justified. What he said next was shocking. He told me that his wife heard her daughter's voice in the midst of the noise. She looked at him and said, "I heard my child, and she does not sound like she is happy." He thought she was just joking around but she was not. They then went downstairs and saw their little girl crying. He was puzzled. "How come I did not hear my child's voice?" he said. Well, only mothers are built like that. A mother can hear her baby's voice from a mile away. Some may call it women's intuition, but I believe that while men and women are both human beings the two are extremely different.

This is why I am always puzzled when I hear single mothers say things like "I have to be both mother and father to my children." This makes no sense. A mother is a woman and she can only be a mother. A father is a man and he can only be a father. Because the mother has to nurse the child and has to show some toughness does not mean that she is now both mother and father. Being tough does not make you a man and being soft does not make you a woman. A man is a man and a woman is a woman. A woman cannot think like a man and definitely, a man cannot think like a woman. We will never think alike. The only way we can know what each other wants is with the use of communication such as talking and writing. Rather, if we are not happy, we have to use our words to let our spouses know how we feel. Clear communication is the most effective method a couple can use to achieve a true union.

There is no quick fix for an unsuccessful relationship. It takes time. Your spouse will understand you and your body in good time. You just have to be patient. Do not rush the process. Warren Buffett, one of the wealthiest men alive, said in a statement, "no matter how great the talent or efforts, some things just take time. You cannot produce a baby in one month by getting nine women pregnant." Allow your spouse to grow with you. Work on the communication process in your relationship and I can guarantee that once both of you have understood the art of communication and how important it is, everything else will fall into place. If you find that your spouse is not forgiving you, then teach him the art of forgiveness. If you see that he is not touching you the way that you want to be touched, then tell him or show him how to touch you.

Finally, if your spouse is talking to you in a manner that you feel disrespected, tell him how you feel and if he doesn't understand then teach him how to speak to you with respect. Remember what I said earlier that he may not be aware of his actions. It is up to you to show love and patience and to inform him and educate him. If he truly loves you then he will most definitely change. Just do not complain to your friends and speak unkindly about your man. This will not change the situation. Do not tell your friends, go directly to your man and tell him how you really feel.

Lastly, I believe that women should be able to voice their feelings. Men should be able to have the rights to voice their feelings as well. It has to go both ways. I found that in my past relationships and also from listening to my friends, that it can be a bit difficult to tell our ladies about the things that they do that hurt us or that make us unhappy. I used to date a lady who was very vocal about her feelings, which was great. I allowed her to feel comfortable and to tell me whatever was on her mind. The minute I told her how I felt she would get angry, or cry. I would have to stop expressing how I felt and embrace her. Sometimes I had to tell her that I was sorry for what I said. I made sure I told her what she was doing that I did not like in a loving manner. This did not help the situation. She was not the type of lady that was ok with hearing that she has faults like everybody else.

After a while, I saw that the relationship was lopsided. That I had to always hold back my feelings for fear she would start crying again. When I say she would cry, I mean that her eyes would swell, and she would moan and groan like I had actually put my hands on her and physically abused her. One would think that I was expressing myself in a combative manner towards her. That could not be more farther from the truth. Sometimes after I had expressed my feelings on what she did that I did not like, I would then think maybe I was overreacting. This was why I would say that I was sorry. No one is perfect, yet she could let me know when I did something wrong but when it came to me telling her, she would get upset and cry to the point of her having headaches afterwards. I then became so used to her crying that I would allow her to finish crying then I would just continue saying what I was saying. I became desensitized to her tears. After a while her tears and her distress meant nothing to me.

I later realized that I was holding back what I had to say so that I could keep the peace and the tears from falling from her eyes. This was the same reason for what pushed me away from her. You will never win when you remain mute. If I had said all the things I wanted to say from the beginning, we would have parted ways earlier in our relationship. However, I held a lot of things in my heart for the sake of keeping the peace and yet we ended up parting ways anyway.

When you hold your peace, the only person you are hurting is yourself. You have been given a mouth with teeth and tongue to communicate with. Please, I say, please use them. This is the only way to relate your wants and needs, and your likes and dislikes to your spouse. If you do not use your voice to express how you really feel, you will then use that same voice to say why you are single and why you cannot find your soulmate. So, having said that, start using your voice as often as you can.

CHAPTER 7
PARENTS

> "The wheel has come full circle."
> – William Shakespeare

"Dreams do come true," Johnathon said, after he purchased his seventeenth apartment building in New York City. He then gave a speech to his team about how he came from a poor background, where he did not have a place to call his own, to a successful real estate investor. After he was finished with his speech, he then raised his wine glass which was half filled with red wine. He looked around the room to make sure everyone's glass was raised so they could toast to his success. He was ready to speak, so he began by saying, "I would like to say," then suddenly he went silent. The wine glass in his right hand began to shake. He started to slowly run his left hand around

through his hair, then around his face in a clockwise motion and stopping at the bottom of his beard.

Everyone was in shock and no one knew what to do. One of his employees walked over to him and she asked, "boss, are you ok?" She then gradually stretched out her hand and took the wine glass from him. "Boss, can you please sit down?" she asked. He sat down and began wailing. While tears were running down his face he looked up and said with a subtle tone, "my wife wants a divorce."

Johnathon had been a single man looking for a lady to call his wife for many years. His employees would always cheer for him whenever he went on a date in hopes that he would find the lady that he deserved. However, he was not a desperate individual. He knew that in order to find a lady, he had to make himself available to meet and spend time with someone and to get to know them. Thus, he did just that. Almost every weekend he went out on a date. Then when he found someone that peaked his interest, he would focus on her and her only. He was not the type of guy that would seek to date multiple women. He was a one-woman man.

Ultimately, he found his queen. She was everything to him and he was everything to her. He loved and cared for her the way a real man should. Some of the women at his office envied the love he had for his wife. They, at times, would compare the love that he had for his wife with the love that their husband had for them and saw that he was showing a lot more love and care to his wife than their husbands were showing to them. His wife did not want for anything. For their vacations, he would take her on cruises, trips to the Caribbean and Europe just to name a few.

Although his job was very demanding, since he was the boss, he would usually take a lot of time off, so he could spend as much time with his family as possible. His wife was a stay-at- home mom so he made sure that when it came to the finances, she was fully involved. She did not have to ask him for money because she knew from the beginning his money was her money as well. What was his was also hers. Besides, he appreciated the fact that she would rather walk away from her career to stay home and nurture their children rather than sending them to daycare.

On the day that he reached one of the major milestones of his career by purchasing his seventeenth building in one of the most expensive cities in the world, his wife's lawyers handed him divorce papers to sign. This was why he was not able to continue his toast. The celebration was finally over and everyone said their congratulations in regard to his success. Johnathon stayed in his office almost the entire day trying to figure out what he had done wrong, in hopes of finding a solution that could easily save his marriage.

According to the story teller, he, at the time did not know why she wanted a divorce. He was confused. He tried to retrace his steps on how he treated his wife since they were married. Nothing came to his memory. So, he did the best possible thing which was to see a marriage counselor. His wife agreed to seeing a counselor and he thought this was a sign of making progress. They went to see a counselor and the question was geared to his wife. "Why do you want a divorce?" Without hesitation, she burst out "he doesn't love me, he doesn't care for me, he doesn't treat me with compassion." Johnathon was totally in shock. He looked at his wife with disbelief. He was rendered speechless.

The counselor then gave Johnathon the floor to say what was on his mind. All he could say was that he was confused. He believed he was a good man, a good husband and great father to his children. He went on to tell the counselor that he always showed her love and that he gave his heart to her and his family, yet he was still confused with the reasons she gave to justify her filing for a divorce. The counselor asked his wife to be specific with her answers. "Please tell me specifically what it is your husband is doing or not doing that is causing you to file for a divorce." She placed her hands over her eyes while crying explosively and said, "he does not make me bleed." Both the counselor and Johnathon were startled by the words she uttered.

Based on her background, she was raised in a small tribe in Africa where at times, men would abuse their spouses and people would turn a blind eye to it. The act of abusing women was the norm to the people of her tribe. It was a way of life that was deeply embedded in their culture. Johnathon's wife told the marriage counselor that her father would physically attack her mother. She said that sometimes her father would punch her mother so hard that her nose and eyes would bleed. Her mother would never complain about being abused. All she would do is head to the bathroom and clean herself up. This was just what would happen in her home when she was a child. Even though her father would attack her mother in such a manner, her parents always made up with smiles, laughter and kisses. The connection that her parents had, according to her, remained strong to the core. She grew up seeing this happen to her mother time after time, on a regular basis, so she thought that this was what true love really was.

The counselor had a one-on-one talk with Johnathon and explained to him why getting a divorce made sense. She told him that his wife wanted a divorce because from her point of view, he was not showing her love like her father showed her mother.

When I heard this story, all I could do was shake my head from left to right with pity for his wife. I believe it is ok to say that she was brain-washed from a very early age. Now in adulthood, her mindset was wired to her past. She was expecting love to be shown to her based on what she was raised to think love was. She couldn't have been farther from the truth. Although Johnathon tried to make it work, he saw that she was neither happy nor satisfied to be with him. Sorrowfully, he signed the divorce papers and they both went their separate ways. Today, his ex-wife is a single woman with an amazing career in medicine, and is still looking for love.

Johnathon was going through a divorce not because he did something wrong, but because of what his wife's mother went through. His mother-in-law did not tell her children that their father was wrong to abuse her. She did not make it clear that love is not about crying because your eyes and mouth are bleeding. She pretended that she was happy in spite of her hurt. Her kids thought that it was ok and that all was well. They grew up believing a lie. The lie that she believed was amplified in her own marriage. She prayed for a wonderful husband and she received what she prayed for. However, he was not exactly what she wanted. Yes, he loved and care for her, but he was missing one ingredient. The ingredient of abuse. She was not tasting her own blood and her face was always perfect without any fist marks or swollen eyes.

This was the reason why a divorce was the only option to solve this problem. She then became a single lady looking for a man. Looking for her king. Hoping that a man, somewhere out there can and will love her like her father loved her mother. Some women are single because what they saw and experienced while growing up lead to false expectations, which is not real for the majority of the world. Parents have to make a conscious effort to live a life of value. They need to show their children what love really is through how they interact with their spouses in the presence of their children. Children need to see their parents going on date night, watching the television together, playing with each other and telling each other how much they love each other.

How could something like this be avoided? I believe that parents are our first teachers. We learn most about life through the life we see our parents live. This is why parents have to be very careful on what they do and say in front of their children because they never know how one single act can affect an entire generation. I know this situation very well. I saw one of my sisters live the same exact life that my mother had lived.

My mother had her first child in her late teens. My sister had her first born in her late teens as well. My mother had three children. One boy and two girls. My sister has three children as well. One boy and two girls. My sisters and I moved to the United States to live with our mother and her new husband in the early '90s. It was not long after my mother was married to her husband that he was laid off from his job. This made my mother the only person with a salary. Even though we did not get the chance to spend as much time with mom, we didn't need for anything.

My mother became a Nursing Assistant. Then she was hired at a hospital where she was trained as a Patient Care Associate. Today, my sister, my mother's first child, also a Nursing Assistant, now works as a Patient Care Associate at a major hospital in Florida. My mother went through a very unhealthy marriage that resulted in her getting a divorce. My sister went through the same exact experience in her first marriage as well, which ultimately led to a divorce. When my mother was alive, she used to work two jobs or she would work a double shift at her job just to make ends meet. Finally, she was able to purchase a beautiful home in Florida. My sister bought her first home in Florida a few months ago. Of course, she used to work two jobs as well. Both women, my sister and my mother, are from totally different generations, yet their lives are identical. They are different people, yet their lives are the same.

How is it that one life was repeated in two generations? Did my sister deliberately copy my mother's life? What if my mother had made different choices, such as staying in school and completing her education? Do you think that my sister would have followed suit? What if my mother had mustered the courage and told her daughter detailed information on why she had a divorce, what wrongs her ex-husband did her or what she allowed him to do to her and the mistakes she had made? Children live what they learn. My sister knew what life was through observing her mother's life. Unconsciously she made choices that mirrored her mother's life, step by step.

My sister must change the cycle for her children to make sure they do not go through the same things and don't have to endure the struggles of life, the struggles that come along with raising a family. Today she is doing just that. My sister is making sure the cycle is broken and remains broken with her generation. She is teaching her children that they are royalty and that when they are looking for a spouse, they should look for someone who values them and treats them with love and respect. She is correcting her mistakes by telling her kids that they need to have patience with people whom they love. She is showing them how they should behave with their spouse, so their spouses will feel loved.

For example, she told her son that he should make sure that whenever his wife is cooking he should, even though he is not a great cook, at least stay around the kitchen and make conversation with his wife while she is preparing dinner for the family. She also told him that he should make salad or juice while his wife is cooking so they could be together rather than having her slave in the kitchen by herself. What caught my attention is that she showed him exactly how to clean the bathroom from top to bottom, so he could be able to help out around the house, especially when his wife gets pregnant. She would not have to bend over to clean the toilet. She would be able to rest her legs when she is in her final stage of her pregnancy and make herself a bubble bath knowing that the bathroom tub is clean.

As a wife, these were some of the things that she was missing in her marriage. Her husband did not show her appreciation like this. She did not get this type of treatment. She was always cooking in the kitchen by herself. All her husband did was eat whatever she prepared for him. He did not have the common courtesy to wash up after himself when he had finished eating. When she was pregnant, she had to clean the house on her own. He would just sit and watch the television or go out for a drink. She was stressed. He did not care that she worked all day on her feet while pregnant with his child and then come home and labor with household chores.

My sister was physically and emotionally abused in her marriage. Her husband abused her because he was weak. He would take out his frustration on her by hitting and punching her like she was a sandbag. At times, her children would see her cry and she would often try to hide her tears from them. She knew that her children were aware of what was going on. So she decided to stop hiding and make a stand. Her stand was not for herself, but for her children. She did not want her children to experience what it feels to be battered and broken.

She did not want her children to constantly taste their own blood like it was part of their diet. Most importantly, she did not want her children to think that it was ok for their spouse to abuse them. To accomplish this, she had to end the marriage. She had to ask him to leave her alone. She did not have the money at first to pay for a divorce lawyer. However, she did her best to save towards it. Eventually, she had enough to hire a lawyer and get her divorce finalized.

She then told her children exactly why she divorced their father. Today, her son knows exactly how to treat a lady. He knows that the only time he puts his hands on his lady is when they are playing or when they are being intimate. He understands the term, "a happy wife equals a happy life." So, his job is to do things that will result in his wife feeling happy versus doing things that would make her unhappy. Her daughters understand that they were not put on this earth as a man's punching bag. They know their worth. They now know that physical abuse is not a form of love. If a man ever were to hit them, they know that that is the end of their relationship with that man. Plus, the authorities would be called to send him to jail.

Neither my sister nor my mother finished college. Having a degree was not a serious topic of discussion in my house when I was growing up. So, my sister did not see how important having a degree from a university was. Today, she sees and understands the value of having an education. She decided to break the cycle and encourages her children to focus on their education. As a single mother of three, she gears her life around her children. She puts her wants and needs on hold while making sure her children are getting ahead as they should. She is actively involved with their studies. She makes sure that their homework is completed before they can watch the television and play. She keeps a constant presence at their schools so their teachers could let her know exactly how her children are doing and how they could improve as students.

Today, her two daughters are doing very well in school. She tends to not get excited when they receive an A on their exams because getting an A is the norm for them. Her son, the eldest child, is working on his second degree and he is not yet 21 years old. He has been an A student from the moment he started attending school. Today, he works as an intern at a major business establishment in Tampa, Florida. As you can see, her children will not repeat the life she lived growing up. She is making sure they begin a new and different cycle in their lives and their future.

We have to understand that children live what they learn. Parents must comprehend that not only what they say can have a significant effect on their children, but also what they do. A lot of what we as humans do is called learned behavior. Most times we are not aware of the things we do because it is so ingrained in our subconscious mind. Here is a quote that can better sum up this chapter:

> "Your beliefs become your thoughts,
> Your thoughts become your words,
> Your words become your actions,
> Your actions become your habits,
> Your habits become your values,
> Your values become your destiny."
> —Mahatma Gandhi

As you can see, your beliefs lead you to your destiny. This is the main reason why I can, sometimes empathize with many single, beautiful, educated, independent women when they explain the reasons for them being single. The beliefs that were taught to them from childhood have crippled their future chances for happiness when it comes to finding a mate. So, it is not always their fault. Sometimes it is their parents fault.

How can we fix this situation? I believe the only way to fix it is through education. I am not talking an institutionalized education, I am talking about education through exposure. This type of education can come in the form of seminars, lectures or meetings in groups where individuals can share their life stories on topics that can open the minds of the attendees to issues and reasons that can and will enable them to have and live the lives that they want. Across the globe, in many countries, states, cities and towns, you can find groups and organizations that focus their attention on helping to solve problems such as this.

Therefore, it would not be difficult to meet others who have already gone through or are currently going through what you may have experienced. The main focus of these organizations is to let you know that you are not alone and that there is help out there. The constant meetings and lectures by women who have been battered and their stories on how they were able to empower themselves to be free from the toxic relationships would eventually empower you to do the same. After a while, you also will be liberated to take immediate actions on your toxic relationship. Then in no time, you would be the one telling your success story, relating what you went through and how you were able to get out of a tough situation.

Another way is through literature. Reading material, like this book, can unmask their old ideas of what they once thought to be the truth when growing up. Once they are willing to open their minds and hearts to welcome new ideas, they will be able to change and adjust to new views about an ideal partner. I do not believe that each issue in this book applies to every single lady. However, I can only hope if a chapter applies to you, that you put it into practice in your life. Just try it out. It never hurts to try. Also, if you know someone with a symptom that this book talks about, you can help to expose them with a copy for themselves. I believe that exposure is key. Just a simple enlightenment can liberate someone from the bondage that has paralyzed their mind and damaged their beliefs.

I have been exposed enough to know how to treat a woman and how a woman is supposed to treat a man. I was very young when my parents were divorced, so I really did not see what happened to make both of them go their separate ways. I heard a lot of chatter but I did not witness anything for myself. However, both of my parents got married again and I was blessed to live with both parents to witness what a marriage should look like.

First, I spent a short time living with my father and his new wife and I can tell you that I saw my father and my stepmother constantly showing love and respect for each other. They were always together. If she was in the kitchen cooking, he was in there tasting the food and talking to her. If he was in the living room watching a soccer match, she would be sitting next to him with her legs on his lap while she was working on her computer. If they were angry at each other, they would go in their bedroom and discuss the problem between themselves. I never heard my father raising his voice to his wife and she never raised her voice to him either. After they finished talking about the issue, whatever it was, they would walk out of the room together and continue doing what they were doing before the issue had occurred.

My father constantly took his wife out to dinner and to places where they could relax and revive their marriage. When they would hug each other, I could tell that they were not acting. It was real because they hugged each other every day. It did not matter where we were, we could be at a five-star restaurant, at church or at our home, once they were eating, they would always end up eating from each other's plate. He had to taste what she was having, and she would complain even though it did not bother her at all. Once she finished cooking, he would tell her how amazing the food was. I could remember my father dancing after his wife made him fried fish. He was so happy and excited for his delicious meal that he had to take his shoes off and dance. My stepmother would smile from ear to ear. I could tell that she felt appreciated. They loved each other, and it showed.

However, my mother and her new husband were the total opposite. I knew that there was no love at all between them. They rarely touched each other and when they did, it seemed to be an act because it did not look real. I could not remember the last time I saw them going on a date. I saw her husband a few times bringing my mother roses and chocolate but that was about it. I remember when the family would go out for dinner, my mother and her husband would always eat from their own plate. She never reached out and took food off his plate and he never did the same. They kept their hands to themselves the entire time.

My mother was very beautiful, yet I do not remember my stepfather telling her how beautiful she was. My mother was the best cook in the entire world.

Everything she made was golden. She could have entered a top chef competition and won with ease. Yet, I cannot recall her husband telling her, in public, how amazing her cooking skills were. I know she knew that she was a great cook, but I believe she would have loved to have heard her husband tell her so every once in a while.

I, Linton C. Samuels, was exposed to two different types of marriages. I know from what I have witnessed, the right way and the wrong way to show love and care to a lady. I am so grateful to have had both experiences. I saw what made a lady's face light up with joy and what can cause a beautiful woman to put her head down and pretend that she was happy. What if I had only lived with my mother and her second husband? I would not know that I should compliment a lady when she walks out of the house looking her best.

I would not know that I should show affection to a woman as often as possible. I would be oblivious to the fact that having an occasional date night is a great way to make a lady happy. The sad part about this is that my mother knew that what she was experiencing was not love, yet she did not sit me down to tell me that her husband was treating her improperly. She knew I saw her pain, yet she remained mute.

To conclude, you have to and must be honest with yourself. If you are being treated unfairly in your marriage, you should voice how you feel with your spouse. Also, if you have children in your home, you should take them aside and explain to them that whatever it was that they have witnessed that your husband did or said to you was not the way real love goes. Let them know from the beginning. After you have told them, then you have to couple that with taking appropriate action. If it means calling the police or making him leave for a few days, you should do it. Let them see that you stood up for yourself by taking an appropriate action. Unlike Johnathon's mother-in-law, she did not tell her daughter that her father was wrong for putting his hands on her. She pretended that she was happy. This was the direct reason why her daughter believed that it was ok for a spouse to abuse her. This false belief is the number one reason why she is still single today. I pray that she one day becomes exposed to literature or some kind of group meeting that could open her eyes to what life really can and should be and eventually cure her of that false sense of belief.

Chapter 8

Walls

> "Better to live on the corner of a roof than share a house with a quarrelsome wife."
> proverbs 21:9

In ancient times, there was a great city called Jericho. Jericho had strong, tall walls coupled with a mighty army. However, it was very difficult to judge how great their army was because their walls always protected them from their enemies. Armies were afraid to fight them. It was a laborious, onerous, and a very burdensome task to get over their walls much less to conquer their city. Joshua, a man of God, who became the leader of his people after the death of Moses, was entrusted with the mission to subdue the city of Jericho. Joshua found out that this was not going to be an easy task.

Jericho's walls were, according to historians, five to six feet in thickness. It was impenetrable. Back then there were no tanks, no sniper rifles, air strikes or grenades to help you. Back in those days, armies did not have the type of equipment to climb walls. Nor did they have the technology to create a machine to destroy such a wall. To get a better example on how the wall of Jericho was, let us think of the wall that surrounds Rome. Although Rome is in Italy, Rome is separated from Italy. Its walls are the separation. The wall of Rome circles the entire city. Everywhere in the city in Rome you can see the wall of protection. Now imagine men with weapons such as stones, fire and bone arrows on top of the walls as well as vats of boiling oil. One would say that it seems very difficult to get to the walls, much less to get over it.

Joshua firmly believed that he could conquer the city of Jericho, so he put faith into action. He toiled and labored day after day. Yet still he saw no sign of a breakthrough. According to the Bible, in the book of Joshua, chapter 6:1 states "now Jericho was completely shut because of the children of the Israel, the army Joshua was leading, none went out and none came in." This means that the same great wall that was preventing the enemy from coming in was also the same wall that held the people of Jericho as prisoners. No one could leave the city for fear of death.

I once typed in the search bar in Google, *beautiful single women.* Above the search bar were menus. I clicked on images and I saw pictures of beautiful single ladies of course. Women from all different parts of the world with different shapes and sizes. Some of these ladies had short hair and some had long silky hair and a few had no hair at all. It did not matter, because they were all beautiful. If I had to take a pick, I would pick all of them. I would be the modern-day Solomon.

I scrolled through a great quantity of pictures and only one picture stood out to me. It had nothing to do with the lady in the photograph, although she was beautiful. What caught my attention was the caption written on the picture. The caption read "my mother taught me how to get a man, but she did not teach me how to keep a man."

This was very interesting. What is preventing women from keeping a man? Is there another answer? If yes, who has the answer? When I was brainstorming ideas for this chapter, I began thinking about the walls of Jericho and how they were built, as well as, how walls are made in general. I came across so much detailed information. Simply put, a wall is made brick by brick and stone by stone. This process continues until the height and width is sufficient to the builder's liking. Sometimes women tend to build a wall around their hearts to protect it from getting hurt. The pain and heartache of a broken heart at times can be so severe that they do their best to protect it by any means necessary. So, they build an emotional wall around their hearts that pushes men away and keeps men at bay; they keep men from getting to their hearts using methods such as complaining, constant fighting, verbal and emotional abuse towards their partners with hopes that they will not be hurt as they were hurt before.

A major brick that contributes to the wall that keeps men away is verbal abuse. It is possible to destroy someone and a relationship with your tongue. The tongue is described as a two-edged sword. It can destroy or create someone. I loved my mother very much. God bless her heart. I remember my father telling me how my mother used to speak to him. Whenever she would get angry, she would say every hurtful word that came into her head and out of her mouth. It was very difficult to believe this at first, as I thought maybe my mother was actually a saint. Well, not a saint, I just saw my mother as a lady who respected men.

Then, all of a sudden, she started to use that same language on me. Immediately at that point I started to believe what my father had told me in the past. When my mom would get upset at me, she would say hurtful things like, "you are good for nothing, you are worthless, I wish you had died in childbirth." All this is just the tip of the iceberg in comparison to the things I heard from my mother while growing up. This actually crushed my self-esteem. I began to doubt myself. Dreams I once had became something of a distant past. These kinds of words were walls preventing me from showing her love the way I wanted to.

The tongue can break you if you are not mentally and emotionally strong. I was in my early teens when I started being verbally abused. I did not know how to handle it. I remember studying for an exam in school and I put forth a great deal of effort trying to get a passing grade for my business law class. When I entered the classroom, I took out my notes to do a quick review. I felt so confident that I put away my review papers and got ready for the exam to begin. The exam finally began. I looked at the test questions with a smile on my face because based on what I saw so far, this test was going to be a walk in the park.

When I was almost finished, I looked over at my neighbor's paper, to my surprise, our answers were totally different. I remembered that she had passed the last exam with a very high score, so I figured that I was the one with the wrong answers. I promptly changed almost all of my answers to that of my neighbor's in hopes of getting a passing grade. When the exam was over, I went to my neighbor and asked her a simple question. I asked her "do you think you passed the exam?" She replied, "no way, I did not study but it's ok I will pass the final." I allowed self-doubt to rob me of a passing grade by thinking that I was inferior and not good enough to pass a simple test on my own. The test results came back and of course my classmate and I both failed the exam. I looked on the answer sheet and saw that had I kept my own original answers I would have gotten at least an A.

I do not blame my mother for instilling self-doubt in my character, however we can at times be the product of our environments. Clearly, I was that product. I must mention that my mother was an amazing woman. She made mistakes and I forgave her a long time ago. I had to work on myself physically, mentally and emotionally. I had to read and build myself up. I started telling myself that I could become the man I wanted to be. I could get what I wanted from this life. I could, and I will be successful. Yes, yes, I could do whatever I put my mind to.

To add, those hurtful words of my mother ultimately pushed my father to believing that he actually was a loser and the he would not have success in life. Thankfully, my father was married a for second time to a woman who used her tongue to create him. She told him how strong he was. She made him feel like he was the smartest guy she had ever met. She believed in his ideas for the future. She used her language to empower him. Today, my father together with his wife own and operate their own business in Jamaica.

My father is the same man. Yet, he became a man of success and happiness because of his wife today. Today he is a successful entrepreneur. However, when he was married to my mother he was just a struggling cab driver working sixteen hours or more per day. I used to cry, as a little boy, because I did not get the chance to see my father as often as I wanted to. Today, he can travel to America and spend as long as he wants to. I can go to Jamaica and we can go to the beach, relax at home or just visit family and friends. He now has the luxury of time and money to do so.

A few years before my mother passed away she and I had become very good friends. We started to spend a lot of time together. Sometimes she would cook and wait for me to come home so we could eat and have a conversation. She then told me why she did some of the things she did. For some reason, I am becoming emotional while writing this paragraph. My mother told me about her past. She told me about some of the rough times she had been through with my father and also at the present time with her current husband. She also went into details about her childhood.

My mother actually opened up to me and told me everything of her past. Now when I think about it, maybe she knew that she was going to die. Maybe she knew that she was gravely ill. All this time I was oblivious to her past hurt. She told me that her father was very abusive to her mom. Her father would beat her mom as often as he could. Her mother decided to pack her things and run away. She ran away for her safety while leaving her children behind. That act broke my mother's heart. She told me that when she was 46 years old. While telling me this, she was crying profusely. After her mom left, there were many events that took place that I cannot mention in this book. However, she carried this pain for 46 years before unburdening herself onto me.

Looking back, I can say that I definitely have forgiven my mother. Now that I know her story, I can understand and see where she was coming from. Although I was verbally abused by her, I can truly say that was not her intention. She did that unwittingly. She was not aware of what she was doing. She pushed me away so many times that I forgot how to hold and hug her. She was pouring her heart out to me and I did not know what to do. I loved my mother, however, I felt withdrawn and disconnected from her. I eventually embraced her. Yet, it felt weird. When she passed away, I remember crying that my mom was gone. Also, I believe that about 80% of my tears were for the simple fact that my mother was living with pain from her childhood for all those years. She was suffering and my siblings and I did not even know. Because we did not know, we could not understand her. For all those years there was a wall of separation between my mother and me. Although I wanted to show love to her, her actions constantly pushed me away and prevented me from getting over her wall of hurt and pain.

Now imagine a man married to a woman who constantly, because of her past heartbreak, verbally abused him. Do you think this man would stay with her? If yes, for how long would he stay? How long would he allow his wife to throw dirt in his face? How long would he allow her to speak down to him and call him disgraceful names? My guess is not long at all. I believe that a marathon and a sprint is different yet very similar. What makes them different is the number of miles for each race. For a marathon, there are 26.2 miles. Whereas a sprint could be a 100- or a 200-meter race.

What makes them similar is that both the marathon and a sprint have a start line and a finish line. Such is life. We start our lives with our birth and we end our lives with death. With that said, a verbally abusive relationship would have to end one day. It has to. That type of relationship would not last. Even if the abuser were unaware of his or her actions. That type of action would still, like the walls of Jericho, separate you from your spouse and eventually push your spouse as far away from you as possible.

My advice to anyone dealing with emotional pain, like pain of a broken heart, abandonment and other emotional pains would be to consult a professional counselor. In order for you to live a happy life, you need to deal with your emotional problems. A few counseling sessions per week or per month could drastically change your mental attitude in a very short while. It may even be deductible under your health insurance plan. You would then draw people to you rather than push them away. The wall of hurt could easily be broken down with just a few sessions with a professional counselor.

Another major brick that contributes to the wall that keeps men away is physical abuse. There are some women who will physically as well as emotionally abuse their men. This is another form of a brick. In the United States and some parts of the world, men tend to go to jail once a woman has physical proof that she has been hit by her man. As a consequence, some ladies tend to physically attack their men knowing they will not harm them in the retaliation and that they may get away with it. This tends to happen when a man shows a sign of weakness, the lady came from an abusive relationship where she was the victim, the lady makes more money, or if the lady is the breadwinner in the home. So, she capitalizes on her opportunity.

Men who are physically abused by women would most likely not come out and talk about it. To them, it is a shame to allow a woman to a physically abuse them. So, they tend to keep quiet about the abuse. Last year a friend of mine sent me a video from YouTube that was very difficult to watch. A couple was in a parking lot arguing. Apparently, the lady thought her husband was cheating. He told her no and that she should calm down. Well, she did not listen to him at all. She began to punch him in his face and in his stomach. Then she slapped him a few times across his face.

He was very patient with her. At one point, he quickly embraced her with a hug and a kiss telling her to stop. Again, she did not listen. She went crazy. She started to kick him multiple times in his legs and stomach area. At one point, I thought that she must have taken self-defense classes, or that Jet Li was her teacher at his karate school, because she was hitting him with various types of combinations. I thought she must have a black belt in karate because she just kept pouring on the hits.

He couldn't talk her into stopping so he decided to walk away and let her cool off. He began to walk away and she ran after him and then continued her attack. This time with a lot more aggression. Based on her facial expressions, it looked like she had allowed her anger towards him materialize into hate. This time, her hits were more deliberate. She was a lot more aggressive than she was in the beginning. It was obvious because the man began to show signs of pain. He started to cover his stomach with one hand and the other he used as a shield to protect himself. Then, his eyes were opening and closing so rapidly signaling that her hits were now taking a toll on him.

After the beating the man was taking, he still mustered the energy to try to walk away. Yet, again the lady came after him. This time he had had enough. He made a fist with his hands and with a few blows to her face she was knocked onto the ground. He was more than half her size and more than a foot taller than she was. The fact that he tried to walk away to avoid getting hurt and control himself from retaliating, which could cause harm to her, actually made sense to me. When I read the comments online, people were more against the man and saying that they would not have put their hands on the woman, and that he was wrong to abuse the poor lady. At one point, I was not sure if they were watching the same video that I was watching.

On November 25, 2009, there was a bear attack at the Berne Bear Park zoo in Switzerland. A 25-year-old man fell into a bear enclosure. The bear quickly attacked the man. The video leaked on social media showing the bear having his way. The bear, hammered his teeth into the man's arm and back and picked him up and carried him like he was meat. Then, the bear began to maul the man with his claws aggressively, biting him in his back, arms and head. Thankfully the police had shot the bear at the opportune time to save the man's life.

Here are my questions, was the bear wrong to attack the man? Maybe the bear had rationalized the situation and thought to himself, "well, this man fell in my cage by accident. Should I forgive him and leave him alone, or attack? I usually will only attack people when they jump into my cage and bother me." Well, this is not how animals think. This is what happened in a nutshell. The man fell in the bear's cage by accident and the bear attacked the man using his animal instinct.

The same with men and women. Women are very good with words when it comes to arguing. Men, on the other hand, will never win a verbal argument with a woman because we would never find the words to compete with them. At times, a woman can verbally and physically abuse a man. Most men would just brush it aside by walking away and trying to ignore them. A man can only take so much. Whether or not a woman was physically and verbally abused or even treated unfairly in her past relationships, it does not give her the right to hurt her man.

Just like the story about the bear and the man. In this case, the man made the mistake of falling into the bear's cage. So, the woman, in the story above, made the mistake of consistently attacking her man with kicks, punches and slaps in the face. The man like the bear, had no choice but to act on his instincts, which was to knock the lady to the ground. To add, based on the zoo incident, people had remorse for both the 25-year-old man and for the bear. The people knew that the bear acted on his animal instincts. However, with the story about the man and his combative fighting wife, people only had remorse for the woman and not the man. I am not saying that it is ok for a man to hit a woman.

It is also not right for a woman to put her hands on a man either. I find it to be a little disturbing when a lady, who has been through a physically abusive relationship, knowing how unhappy she was in the relationship, somehow is able to liberate herself from that toxic situation, only to become the abuser in her next relationship. She takes advantage of her spouse not because she wants power, but to take the power away from him in hopes that he would submit to her and not mistreat her as had happened to her in her previous relationships. Being this aggressive towards a spouse is never healthy. Most men would not live like this.

Does this make sense? What about forgiveness and moving on? I believe that it is human nature to protect ourselves from harm and danger. We should not just assume that danger is coming because we saw danger in the past. When we live life always on the defensive, we tend to be more aggressive than we should, and as a result, we push people away from us. If we are always thinking that someone is going to hurt us, then we will constantly hurt the ones who love us.

I almost put my hands on a woman. She was actually pushing me to my breaking point. She argued and complained constantly. That was not the problem. The problem was the fact that she would get in my face and actually say every word possible to break me. Thankfully, I found an escape. Whenever we had intense arguments, most of the time I would depart from that location and return hours after. I will not put my hands on a woman. When we finally broke up, I remember her telling me that she was surprised that I did not run after her and try to get her back. I laughed in my head. The constant arguing, and her pushing me to use my hands on her, actually destroyed the love I once had for her. When I look back at that relationship, knowing what I know now, I can tell that maybe she had some unresolved issues going on in her life that I was not aware of. This led her to say and do certain things. Nonetheless, it does not justify her actions.

Another brick that contributes to the wall that keeps men away, is called "The Wall of Complaints." Some ladies love to complain about everything. It's too hot, it's too cold, it's too long, it's too short, it's too far, or it's too near. This is definitely a form of a brick. Most men, well the good ones, will try their best to please the love of their lives. Although, when they see that it is impossible to do so, then they find ways to appease themselves. There is a sentence in the Bible that states, "it is better to dwell in the corner of the housetop, than with a contentious woman in a whole house."

I used to work with a guy by the name of John. He was arrested for having a large amount of marijuana in his possession. He said it was not his but that is beside the point. He was taken to a holding cell for a few days. While he was in his cell, he saw a well-dressed man in a suit and tie sitting on the floor. His head was in between his legs with his hands on the top of his head. His shoes looked shiny and glossy, which meant he took pride in his appearance. The man sat like that all day.

He was wrongfully arrested. He went home from a hard day of work and before he could change his clothes and relax, his wife just began to complain. Both of them began to argue. It got to the point where the police were called, and he was arrested. His wife lied and said that he hit her. Later however, he was free to go. Exactly what transpired still remains a mystery to me but what follows speaks volume.

An officer came to the cell and told the guy in the suit that he was free to go. The man stood up, then walked towards the officer. With tears in his eyes, he asked, "can you please give me a few more days in here, please I am begging you." In shock the officer replied, "why would you want to stay in here for another day?" The well-dressed man lifted up his head and said, "because I do not want to go home to her." When he said her, he was referring to his wife.

He would rather sit on the floor of a jail cell than to go home to a warm bed with pillows, sheets, a mattress and a comforter. He rather use a toilet that is filthy with urine stains on it while officers and other inmates were watching him, than to use the toilet in his master bathroom where he would have ultimate privacy. He would rather have peanut butter and jelly with water than have a nice warm meal of his choosing at his house. This was how bad it was for him. He was so quick to call jail his home rather than go home to the lady he married. How sad is that? He said that he had a better night's sleep on the floor of his cell than he had been able to get at home for many years.

We men are not used to constant arguing and complaints. If you notice that your husband delays coming home every night, you should ask yourself what you are doing that is preventing him from coming home to you. You need to be truly honest with yourself. When you find out what it is that you are doing, then you can choose to keep doing it and live with the fact that your husband would rather stay out late than come home to you or you can change your behavior. When my friend told me the story about the man in jail, I laughed. I thought it was funny. As a matter of fact, I thought he was just telling a joke. I quickly believed that story because shortly after, my good friend, a guy I consider to be my brother, called me on his way home around 7pm. We were on the phone talking about sports amongst other things. A few hours went by and I looked at the time and it was after 1am.

I was shocked because I had worked that morning. I told him the time and he said that he knew what time it was. He said that he was home all along but that he was in his car talking to me. I asked him why hadn't he gone inside. With a long pause, he said, "I want to wait until she is sleeping." I did not know that he was unhappy. I did not know that she argued that much. She looked like a saint, yet when she was home she became a devil. Here is what was shocking to me: It was cold outside, yet he would rather stay in his car than go inside his house. You have to understand that arguments are bricks that build very tall, very thick walls. These walls are putting a separation between you and your spouse. Yes, he would try to make it work because he loves you but sooner or later, if you do not break down those walls by stopping your incessant complaining, he may very well give up and another woman would take your place.

    I am certain that men in this life will never really understand women. Most times, we men are confused as to what women want. Some women complain if her man is out of work. When the man finds a job, the lady complains that he works too much and that he does not have time for her. Here is a quick note, a man who works 40 to 60 hours a week cannot be around his woman 24 hours a day. However, a man without a job can. In today's society, there are a lot of ambitious hardworking women. Some of these women complain that they do not have the time to cook dinner because by the time they get home they are tired. So, the man would understand and make dinner for the family. Sadly, his lady would come home and complain that what he cooked was not what she wanted to eat and that she had made plans to cook dinner because she loves to cook for her family. This makes no sense.

I have heard ladies on many occasions, say that they think their husbands are having an affair because they do not have sex with them as much as they used to. Then I hear them say that their husbands must see them as sex objects because they constantly want to have sex. A man listening to all these complaints would one day give up. This is a lot of complaints for one man. This would eventually push a man away from his wife. All of these complaints would stack up, one on top of the other and could eventually become as high as the walls of Jericho, which would keep your man at bay.

The sad part about the story of the well-dressed man in the jail cell, was the simple fact that the man still loved his wife despite not wanting to rush back to his home after getting arrested for something he did not do. Today in the United States, if a lady called the cops and claimed that you hit them, you would be sent to jail. He loved his wife. However, he found comfort in a jail cell. Do not get me wrong, there are men who do indeed mistreat women. I am talking about the faithful men that love and respect their spouses.

When I see women treating men like this I can sympathize with these women. It is because they have been through so much hurt. They previously gave their hearts to men and their hearts were directly and intentionally broken. So, the next best thing to do is to protect themselves, to protect their hearts from ever splitting in two again. They wear their emotions on their sleeves. With the bitter taste of a heartbreak that is coupled with anger, they make the next guy feel their pain. Although they are still looking for love, they cannot seem to let the hurt go. So instead, they build a wall, stone by stone and brick by brick of fighting, arguing and constant complaining just to name a few.

Jericho's city wall was so massive and great that the enemy could not get in. Yet, that same wall, the same wall that protected them from the enemy, also held them as prisoners in their own city. Ladies, when you build a wall around your heart, around your feelings and emotions, by treating men a certain way, what you are doing is actually preventing someone from loving you. You are literally preventing a man from treating you like a queen. You are keeping a possible man-of-your-dreams mute, based on your actions so he would not be able to ask you to marry him. Lastly, you are keeping a man from loving you, which will ultimately prevent you from loving someone. There is a song that we sing at my church that says,

> Love is something that you give away and it comes right back to you.
> It is just like a magic penny, you put it in your pocket and you don't have any.
> (Meaning it has disappeared)
> But if you take it and give it away, it comes right back to you.

With that said, you have to forgive and let go of your past. Once you keep that wall around your heart, I can assure you your heart will not get broken. Sadly enough, you would be unloved. Or worse, you will not love again. So just let go and cut out the constant arguing for no valid reason. Stop with the complaining and the fighting just has to stop. Once you have broken down the wall of your past, you will automatically take down the bricks we have spoken about. Your heart will be able to love again. Also, love will then return to you.

Chapter 9
Burn It

> "To guarantee success,
> act as if it were impossible to fail."
> -Dorothea Brande

Hernán Cortés was a Spanish Conquistador. He pulled off one of the ultimate victories in world history. He took his army on ships to the enemy's shores. After his men unloaded their ships, he had them spy out the land to see what they were up against. To their surprise, they were outnumbered. Some researchers claim that they were outnumbered by about ten to one. This brought doubt and fear into the hearts of his men. They believed that it was not possible for them to be victorious against such odds. So, they were trying to find ways to retreat. Finally, they came up with an amazing solution. The solution was to go back on their ships, head home to regroup and recruit more men so victory could be theirs.

Cortés was not fond of the idea of going home to regroup. He then, with faith, took drastic steps to make sure that retreating was not an option. While his men were resting on the sea shore one night, he asked a few of his faithful followers to assist him on an important task. They overwhelmingly agreed. He instructed them to set their ships afire. His men were confused for a few minutes and hesitated, hoping that their leader would actually change his mind or explain the task further. Hernán Cortés just stood there and said, "burn all of our ships." His obedient followers then did just that.

The smoke from the burning ships was so strong that it woke up the rest of the troops from their sleep. They woke up to a bitter sight. Some were angry while many were confused as to why Cortés set their ships on fire. One of his men cried out, "now how are we going to get home?" Hernán Cortés told his men that regrouping was out of the picture. He said, "we can win this battle, or we will perish here." The same soldier again asked the question, "how are we going to get home if our ships are at the bottom of the ocean?" Cortés looked the soldier in the eye and said, "we will go home on our enemy's ships."

Although they were outnumbered they won the battle. They won the fight yet they doubted themselves.

Dorothea Brande wrote a book entitled, *Wake up and Live*. She stated, "to guarantee success, act as if it were impossible to fail." Once you have put yourselves in a position that failing is not an option, you would be surprised at how powerful you are. You would find out that you have internal strength that is far more than what you thought you had. What Hernán Cortés did in 1519 was remarkable. He put his men into a live or die situation where their survival instinct kicked in and helped them create all possible ways to succeed. Let's face it, they had no other choice. Their ships were in flames and their only means of getting home was on their enemy's ships.

How often do we, as individuals, place ourselves in positions where we have no choice but to be successful? In Hernán Cortés' case, he had to literally burn his ships to guarantee himself and his men victory. These ships were tangible, valuable and visible. Most of the time, we have ships within ourselves that can hold us back from what we want most. These internal ships are what I call behavioral ships. Like Cortés, we have to and must burn them in order for us to get the love and happiness that we want in or relationships. Burning these behavioral ships will force us to destroy our bad habits and create new and more productive ones.

Ladies, what kind of a man are you looking for? Please ask yourselves this question: You have to be a hundred percent true to yourself. There is a quote that says, "to myself be true." Being true is the first and most important step in every aspect of life. Get a piece of paper and write down exactly what you are looking for in a man. Make sure it is detailed information so that if someone were to take that piece of paper and go shopping for that person for you, you would not be disappointed with the man the person brings.

Remember the story of Hernán Cortés. He was willing to go to great lengths to get what he wanted. He destroyed with fire whatever the obstacle was or had the potential to hold him back. Now ask yourself what it is that is holding you back from getting that spouse that you are looking for. As I said before, you have to believe that what you are looking for is also looking for you because that is almost always true. So, you have to, in a sense, become who or what you are pursuing.

Now let's get to the meat of this topic. A lady once told me that she was looking for a man who could speak to her with respect even when he is angry at her. Also, she said that she would love to have a man who could correct her with love rather than telling her that she has done something wrong in such a way that makes her feel stupid or worse, like a child. That was the first on her list of what she wants from a man. Then I asked her, "when you are angry, do you raise your voice and yell at individuals when you are talking to them?" She said, "yes." Then I asked her a follow up question, "do you think that the man you are looking for is searching for a lady who would disrespect him with her words? She said, "no." So, I asked her, "then how do you think you would ever find a man like that?" I told her that the only way she could find a man like that is if she were to burn her behavioral ship, which in this case, is her disrespectful way of speaking to a man.

Communication is one of the keys to having a successful relationship. The sad part about this is that communication is a skill that most people take for granted. We tend to overlook it without knowing how important it is. We do not take enough time to learn and master the art of communication as much as we should. Yet we blame each other for not communicating to ourselves the proper way even though we ourselves do not have the slightest clue on how to communicate correctly.

An old friend once told me how to communicate and relay my message to anyone without the individual feeling disrespected or hurt. The communication method is called the sandwich method. The sandwich method begins with something positive about the individual which is called the bread and then the issue you have with the person, which is called the meat. Then reinforcing the positive things you said about the person is the other slice of bread.

For example, your spouse has walked in the house with a nasty attitude. He is upset because something went wrong at his job and his manager wants to put the blame on him even though it was not his fault and the situation was out of his control. So, your spouse walks in and sees you watching the television and there is no food on the stove and no food on the table and he is famished. He then walks over to you and begins to yell at you with an extremely amplified tone telling you how you are a lazy woman and that you knew the time he was coming home and you did not prepare anything for him to eat or at least ordered take out for him.

The average person would react to this situation in a like manner. Now, by doing this, both of you would just be yelling at each other and who knows what this could escalate to. The sandwich method would be the correct method of choice in this circumstance. Here is how this method would work in this situation. Just think how you make a regular sandwich. First you have a slice of bread, then you put the meat on it and then you place the other piece of bread on top to complete the sandwich. This is a very simple process. Now let us see how the sandwich method would devolve the situation that was given in the example above.

Number one, you begin with the first piece of bread. The bread can be something positive or something reinforcing that could ease the tension. For example, you may say to him, "honey, I know that you love me very much and this is not the way you usually speak to me. You have always spoken to me with love and respect, so I will forgive you before you tell me that you are sorry. This is why I will never hold this against you." By saying something like this, you are changing the mood of the situation. You are actually controlling the outcome of the situation by telling him that you see how he is behaving and you know that this is unlike him. There is a text in the bible that says, "Be not overcome of evil, but overcome evil with good" and "perfect love casteth out fear." When the first thing that comes out of your mouth is good and loving, your spouse would most likely calm down and think about what it is that you have to say. Would this always happen? No. Most of the time it will be able to work especially if the person is in love with you.

Number two is the meat. The meat is the core of the problem. This is where you let your spouse know how you really feel. Now that you have your spouse's attention after you have calmed him down, you can tell him how rude he was behaving. For example, you say, "please, never talk to me like that again because I am not your child and I do not work for you. I do not appreciate and won't tolerate this type of behavior. Respect goes both ways so if I have to respect you then you have to respect me." If you were to say these words at the beginning while he was yelling at you, I am most certain that he would not pay you any attention. Both your voice and his would just sound like noise in the house. This would not get you guys anywhere. It would only worsen the situation.

Number three is the final ingredient to completing the sandwich method. This bread is where you reinforce your first statement. You can tell him that you understand that he is going through a lot of stress at work and that his boss is in the wrong for trying to blame him for something he did not do. You can let him know how much you understand where he is coming from, again, in a loving manner, and maybe help him find a solution to fix the problem.

Let me make this crystal clear. If you are not that person that defuses an argument by the use of good communication skills, then this would be difficult for you. This is something that takes time to get used to. Mastering the art of communication will not happen overnight. However, it is a skill you should work on. At times, having to be the one to take the high road in order to change the mood of a situation can be burdensome. It is easier to take the other road, which most people would in this case, the road to defend one's self by yelling and screaming at the other individual. Sometimes the road less traveled is the road to take. This road can lead to happiness. Taking this path can eventually change your life for the better.

So, now you ask yourself, "Do I want my spouse to try his best to use proper methods of communication and to relate his message to me about how he feels, letting me know what I have done wrong in a loving and kind way?" If your answer is, "yes," then you should look deep inside of yourself and see whether or not you are that same type of person. If you are a lady who would yell and scream at the top of her lungs and use words that can emotionally hurt her spouse, then you should do your very best to burn that type of behavior. You would definitely need to burn that behavioral ship.

You have to and must become the type of woman that your ideal man is searching for. You may think that you can be who you are based on your good looks, ambition and career and that you can still get any man that you want. Of course, you could get any man that you want. We men love beautiful women. As a matter of fact, we love women, period. So yes, you would be able to get a man. The next step is to keep him. Real men want to be respected especially if they do their very best to talk to their ladies with love and kindness.

A man who does his best to honor his lady knows that being respectful with his words are very important to having a long-lasting relationship. So, your beauty can get him. Your disrespectful ways would scare him away. After he leaves you, you would be back to square one complaining that it's difficult to find your soulmate. When really it is not difficult at all. All you have to do is burn your behavioral ship that is holding you back from having a happy, loving life and you would be surprised as to what comes next.

Do you want a man to think it is ok for you to speak to him in a rude manner and expect he will not get upset? I do not think that you would want what is called a "push over" of a man to call your husband. A push over is a man who allows a woman to tell him what to do, tell him to shut up, yell at him, treat him like he is stupid, and at home and in public feel comfortable in disrespecting him in front of strangers, friends and families. This is a man who is so afraid of his lady or of losing his lady that he allows this type of treatment. Is this the man you are searching for? I believe the answer is, "no." You must become what you are looking for. So, you are looking for someone to speak to you with love and respect. You must believe that the ideal man you are looking for is also looking for a soulmate who will speak to him with love and respect as well. You have to become what you are looking for or else what you are looking for will not be able to find you.

Now, let's say that on that piece of paper entitled "the spouse I'm looking for," you write down patience. You believe that the guy you marry must be able to be patient with you. That is a good trait to have because patience is a virtue. The dictionary describes patience as an ability or willingness to suppress restlessness or annoyance when confronted with delay. Do you think that a man who mentally chooses to exercise patience would actively seek out a lady who is impatient? I hope that your answer is "no." Having said that, ask yourself this question, do I have patience? If your answer is "no," then you have to burn the impatience out of your life. That behavioral ship can also keep you away from finding and keeping your ideal spouse.

I once went on a dating site and I was viewing a lady's profile. I found her profile to be very interesting. In the section that states what are you looking for, she wrote that she is looking for a man that is very fit, toned, in shape and is serious about his health. Here is the funny part of her profile. In most of her pictures she was eating unhealthy foods and she was looking like she was about 50 pounds overweight. Come on, she cannot be serious about what she wants. I'm not trying to make fun of obese women because I believe that we are all beautiful no matter of our different skin color, shape, size, weight and height. However, I do believe that we have to and must become what we are looking for.

A person who is all about diet and exercise at times would have the tendency to be attracted to someone with similar interests. For example, I am a bit overweight and doing my best to eat healthfully and exercise as much as I can. I must tell you the truth, it is very difficult to stay on the healthy path. It takes a lot out of me just to get out of my bed and go for a quick jog. While jogging, I would tell myself my goal is to do three miles. Then when I reach two miles, I begin to tell myself that there is no way I can do three miles because I am so out of breath, or, my mind is just not strong enough to help me pull through and finish what I have started. I would then head back home, take a shower and go back to my comfort zone, which is my bed.

Today, I am a single man looking for my queen. What am I looking for? I am looking for a woman who is adventurous. A woman I can work-out with and can keep me accountable for eating right. I am looking for a woman who is health conscious and cares about her body, inside and out. If that individual is also active and trying to eat properly we then can help each other. Say I was to date someone who is not into exercising and eating right. We would have a lot of problems. I would want to wake up to go for a run, and she would get angry that I'm leaving the house so early or I'm not spending enough time with her.

I might want to go to the gym, but no, she would complain that I'm spending too much time away from her because she does not see the value in exercising hence she would not come with me. To make matters even worse, if I were to consistently ask her to join me at the gym, she could possible think that I am calling her fat. That is the worst that can happen. Her thinking that she is fat could spiral downward very quickly. It can go from believing that she is fat, to her feeling that I think that she is not sexy, to her feeling insecure with her body and into her thinking that I am cheating on her with an attractive woman from the gym. By this time, our relationship is bound to come to an end, even if she were not overweight or obese.

Additionally, when we would go out to eat, she would have a problem because I would want to stay away from fatty foods such as fries, pizza, fried foods, salty foods and sugary foods as much as possible. Problems would be bound to occur. I am not saying that every time we go out that I have to eat healthfully, or she eats unhealthful. I am basically saying that for the most part I would prefer to eat healthfully about eighty percent of the time. Do you see how issues can occur in a relationship if both parties are not on the same page? So, if you are looking for a man who is all about eating healthfully and taking care of his body, then you have to ask yourself a simple question. Is this healthy eating exercising man looking for someone who is also healthy and trying to get in shape? If your answer is "yes" then you must ask yourself another question. "Am I doing my best to eat right and get into shape?"

If your answer is "no" then you ought to know what you have to do. You have to start eating healthfully and doing exercises that can burn fat off your body which will get you in shape. You will also have to burn your behavioral habits. In this case, it is your unhealthy eating habits. You are going to have to burn the late-night eating and heavy sugary drinks from your diet. You have to prepare your body for your ideal man while he prepares his body for his ideal lady. And yes, you are that ideal lady.

Another example of a behavioral ship is what I call an un-Christian like behavior. I hear women say that they would love to find a truly Christian man. I believe that women searching for a truly Christian man know that a man trying his best to live by the word of God comes with benefits. Here are some benefits that come with having a truly Christian man in your life:

Number one, a truly Christian man would not commit adultery. Yes, no one is perfect, however a man who is doing his best would understand that adultery is a sin against God and that according to the bible, adulterers will not make it into the kingdom of heaven. So, you can rest assured that you most likely would not have the headache of finding out that your husband is cheating on you. Or worse, you would not find out that your husband has fathered a child outside of your marriage. This is one pain that I do not wish on any woman. My sister and my mother have both experienced the heartache and the bitterness of finding out that their husbands committed adultery and fathered children with other women. I have seen the hurt and pain in those women's eyes. This betrayal can be a bit overwhelming. It could get to the point where the minute he leaves the house to go to work or even to the store, you begin to think that he is going to another woman's bed. Doing this can destroy your self-esteem and damage yourself worth. So yes, being with a Christian man would mostly eliminate this from your life.

This truly Christian man would know that it is best to avoid situations where he could be tempted to cheat on his wife. Like going to clubs, dancing and making physical contact with other women, having constant loose sexual conversations and flirting, just to name a few, would not be a part of his lifestyle. As I said earlier, no one is perfect. There is a possibility that your spouse can make a mistake if he is not strong enough. However, if he were to make it part of his regular routine to follow God and be the truly

Christian man he ought to be, the chances of him falling into another woman's bed would drop significantly.

Number two, a truly Christian man would not take his pay check to the casino and gamble it away. This is definitely not a characteristic of a man who is doing his best to follow the word of God. This man would take his pay check home for his wife and his children. He would put his family first because that is one of the things that God requires him to do. He would make sure that there is food in the house, so his family can be properly nourished. For certain, there would be light in his home so his children could read and study for school. This man would take care of the car payments and make sure the family car has gas in the tank so that he and his wife could go to their destinations without any problems. A truly Christian man like this would think about himself after he has taken care of his family. To note, this is what it means to be truly Christian. Putting others first just like Jesus did by dying for us. That is how much He loved us and that is the same love he requires husbands to have for their wives. Only a truly Christian man would know this and practice it in his daily life.

The sad part is that not everyone who attends church is a true Christian. This is a given fact. Going to church nowadays has become a form of tradition or an event for many individuals where we dress in our most beautiful attire and walk into church every weekend because our parents and our parent's parents went to church in their day. Now, it is like we have to continue the tradition. We can go to church as often we want, but if God is not in us then we are just wasting our time. As I said, a true Christian is a person who is willingly doing his or her best to follow God to the best of their abilities. Whether or not this individual behaves perfectly, his main purpose in life is to love and obey the word of God.

    Now ladies, you say that you want a man that is a true Christian. I want you to actually examine your life and ask yourself if your own lifestyle is that of a true Christian. You have to be honest with yourselves. You can ask yourself, "do I love attending clubs and allowing other men to touch me inappropriately?" If the answer to that question is "yes," then you have to get rid of that type of behavior. In other words, you have to burn that behavioral ship. One thing could lead to another. A touch could lead to a smile. Then a smile could lead to flirting. Flirting could lead to contact information being exchanged. Before you know it, you could wake up with shame for having sexual interaction with a man who is not your husband. If you are looking for a man who will not allow something like this to happen, then you yourself have to burn this type of behavior so when you find your ideal mate you would not do something like this to him, which could eventually destroy your relationship.

Additionally, a truly Christian man would make it his duty to take care of the finances by making sure that all the expenses are paid on time and that his family is never in need of anything. Here is my question to you, do you set your finances in order by budgeting your income or do you just spend your money very loosely without a care in the world? If you are one of those ladies who loves to spend money and keep up with the latest fashion trends rather than saving and paying your bills on time, then you can expect trouble with your ideal spouse.

Money is one of the main reasons why many marriages are destroyed. When one person wants to budget and limit spending to save for the future, while the other person just wants to spend loosely without conscience, problems will definitely follow. Both individuals must be on the same page. If you find that you have a spending problem, you should seek help to eliminate it from your life and allow your spouse to handle the financial aspect of the relationship. It is a gruesome sight to see the bank putting a foreclosure sign in front of a home where a mother and father live with their children. That is not a pretty sight. Also, it is so embarrassing to see a tow truck towing your vehicle while your neighbors or your coworkers are watching just because you are bad at money management which caused you to miss a few car payments.

This can cause a lot of stress in the relationship. The constant fretting and worrying about where the family is going to sleep and where the next meal is coming from could affect how the married couple treat each other. Bitterness, anger, disdain and hate could easily take over the couple. Eventually this could cause them to go their separate ways.

Here is how you can fix this problem: There is a famous phrase that we all know that says, "prevention is better than the cure." To solve this problem, you would have to get in front of it. You can get in front of this problem by doing a self-evaluation and being true to yourself. If you find that you are not too financially literate, then you should sit down with your spouse and make your spouse be in charge of the finances. If you are single and looking for a husband, then you should now begin to learn how to save and monitor your spending. Learning financial responsibility is a great way to burn your bad spending habits. Having this skill would set you up for a successful marriage versus not having it, which would lead you down the path to marital problems and a possible divorce.

By now you should be able to see that by burning your behavioral ships, you are actually preparing yourself for what you want. More so, you are preparing yourself for what you are going to receive. So, by setting these behavioral ships such as impatience, disrespect, overeating, bad eating habits and the lack of exercise and bad spending habits on fire, you are actually doing as Dorothea Brande says you should do; that is, "to guarantee success, act as if it were impossible to fail." Indeed, this is an act of faith. Rather than sitting and complaining that it is difficult to find the right guy, you are taking action by working on yourself; you are preparing you for what you are looking for.

There was a story about two farmers. Both farmers prayed for rain. Yet only one farmer went out and prepared his field for a possible harvest by breaking ground and sowing seeds. Here is the question, which of the two farmers had faith? The answer is obvious. The farmer who went out and prepared for what he prayed for is the one who had faith. Preparation is the key that unlocks every door that needs to be opened in order for us to get what we need and to reach our goals.

To sum up, search yourself and find out all of the behavioral ships in your life that are holding you back from finding the spouse that you are looking for. Then after you have found them, please do yourself a favor by setting them on fire. It does not matter how big or small they are. You have to burn them. Some of you reading this chapter might believe that it is easy for you to burn your ships. I believe that some of the behavioral ships we have in our lives are very easy to get rid of. Yet, if they are so easy to get rid of, then why do we still have them in our lives?

Here is the answer. What is easy to do is also easy not to do. It is very easy to make a healthy salad for dinner. However, rather spend more time making French fries and burgers for dinner. It is easy for most people to walk one mile a day, but it is also easy not to do that. It is easy to say I am sorry and it is easy not to say that you are sorry. Just saying that it is easy is not enough. You have to do that easy thing. Now you may have some ships out at sea that need to be set on fire. Yes, some of them are easy to get to and some are a bit difficult to reach. Well, how about you burn the ones that are the easiest to reach first and rest assured while you are burning your behavioral ships, the guy you are looking for is also doing the same thing. He will be preparing himself for you while you prepare yourself for him. So, when you guys meet, your relationship could take off like a plane and reach its ultimate altitude.

You are reading this book because I have burned my ships. I should have already completed this book a long time ago, but I did not. I allowed my ships to keep me from finishing this book. These ships were procrastination, laziness, doubts, the television, social media, friends, family, practicing the piano and the burden of having too many goals. I had to really find out what was the reason for why I was not finishing this book. Well, I finally found it. As soon as I found the reasons I went to work. I started to burn procrastination first by setting small goals for the book. For example, I would make sure to write approximately seven paragraphs a day. This was easy to do but I was not doing it. Some weeks would go by and I did not even write one paragraph because it was also easy not to do it.

I found out that once you begin to create good habits then everything else will fall into place. I began to program myself to write seven paragraphs a day and I made it my duty to write those seven paragraphs. Then suddenly,

I started to write nine paragraphs. Then ten paragraphs. Writing started to become a part of my routine that I forgot to practice the piano. It got to the point where I could not find the remote for my television because I had been so busy writing that I forgot to watch the television. Someone asked me for my Instagram name and I totally forgot because it has been that long since I have been on that social media application. My friends started to say that I have abandoned them. This was true because if I was not at work, I was in my apartment writing. I can remember writing about 15 paragraphs before I went to bed and waking up early to pick up where I left off.

    Can you believe this? All I did was set one of my ships on fire. That ship was procrastination. For some miracle, there was a strong wind that blew some of the debris particles from that burning ship to the other ships which caused them to burn and eventually sink. So, there is a cure after all. The fact that you are reading this book is a testament that all of my behavioral ships have been turned to ashes. I gave myself all of the fuel I needed to be successful. I did not retreat by waking up late to stay in my comfort zone and watching the television. I refused to take a full-time shift at my job because I believed that I had the ability to become a best seller.

I knew that as a full-time worker I would be given better health benefits than that of a part-time worker. I would be guaranteed a full paycheck every week where as a part-time worker, without notice, I could be told that my days will cut but I did not care. I had to act as if it were impossible to fail. I choose to work a part-time schedule which gave me the flexibility to work only when I wanted, so I could put more of my time and energy into writing and marketing this book. This published book is my proof.

As this chapter comes to a close, I would like you to pick one thing that you do that has the potential of keeping you from finding your ideal spouse or from successfully keeping your spouse in your life. Please, I must repeat, you have to be totally honest with yourself. Remember that in life, that we are part of the solution and part of the problem. Just pick one of your behavioral ships and do your best to burn it. Trust me, your entire life will change. It worked for Harnán Cortés. It worked for me. I believe that it will definitely work for you as well.

Conclusion

I have written nine chapters on the issues that women are facing today that cause them to be single. They are entitled Love, Speak Up, Availability, Fear, Parents, Traditions, The Wall, Changing and Burn It. Every chapter is important to solving the "I am single and I can't find or keep a good man" epidemic. However, I believe that there is one chapter that is the cure all. This chapter can and will change every situation for the good. This chapter is entitled Love. Love conquers everything. Love is pure. This is why I made Love to be chapter one, so it can set the tone for the entire book.

Number one, the Speak Up chapter, encourages women who are being mistreated by their men or are not happy in their relationships to voice how they feel to their spouses. This chapter focuses on them expressing themselves for themselves. I believe love begins with you, as an individual first. The individual can show love to someone else. There is no way a lady can say that she loves herself yet allows her spouse to treat her like garbage. If she loves herself, then she would speak up and let her man know how she really feels and what she truly wants. As discussed in the Love chapter, patience is one of the major characters of love. This means that after you have spoken to your spouse about how you would like him to speak to you and to touch you, for example, you would have to exercise patience with him.

If he truly loves you then he would do his best to change his old habits. We now understand that love is an action word. When you see him trying to change his ways then that is a much stronger sign that he loves you rather than his taking you out to a fancy restaurant or buying you a silk purse. Here you can see, both of you are showing love to each other. You are showing him love by being patient and understanding with him and he is showing you his love for you by respecting you enough and by doing the things that will make you happy, which is why you must learn to speak up and let your voice be heard.

Number two, the Availability chapter, talks about the lady making time in her very busy schedule and getting to know someone. It does not matter if you go to school full-time, work full-time and have a family, you must make yourself available to spend time with someone. No one is an island, no one stands alone. If you love yourself, then you owe it to yourself to share that love in your heart with someone. You will not be able to know whether or not a man has the characteristics of love within his heart if you do not make yourself available to him and get to know him.

When you are looking for a spouse you should remember that what you ask you shall receive. What you seek you will find. In this case, when you make yourself available to find love, love will then come to you. Just remember Ruth. Remember how much she always put herself in positions for Boaz to take note of her. Although she was a bread-winner for herself and her mother-in-law, when Boaz asked her to dinner she would always make time for him. By doing this, she was able to get married and have a family. In order to have love, joy and happiness, you have to go out there and search for it. Men are the hunters and women are the prey. In order for a man to hunt a woman, she must make herself a prey for men to hunt or else men will just go hunting elsewhere.

Number three, the Fear chapter, speaks to taking a chance. One of my favorite quotes states "there is no fear in love; but perfect love casteth out fear: because fear hath torment. He that has fear is not made perfect in love." As covered in the Fear chapter, you must take a chance on yourself. You must love yourself enough to exit a toxic relationship when it is giving you nothing but pain and suffering. If a guy is constantly cheating on you and physically and emotionally abusing you, you have to do something about that relationship.

The sooner you fix the relationship or exit the relationship, the sooner you can move on with your life. If you constantly allow your spouse to abuse you then you would eventually become a slave to your spouse. You would then believe that your body is a piece of meat to be used for sex and to be used as a punching bag. This is why you cannot afford the fear of "the unknown" to hold you back. You have to love yourself enough to walk through the gates of uncertainty. You have to believe that there is hope beyond the gates and allow yourself to move on with your life. You have to believe that if you were to leave your abusive relationship that you would find love and happiness once you have taken that leap of faith and walked through the gates. You have to love yourself enough to quickly change or put an end to a relationship that is giving you nothing but pain. The quicker you put a stop to that relationship, the sooner you will be able to move on and find an individual who would love you and treat you like the queen you are.

Number four, the Traditions chapter, speaks of a way of life which society teaches. As mentioned previously, you should not seek a man just because he possesses material things, such as a degree from a university or that his income is sufficient to meet your needs. You must look within a man and find out who he really is. You have to take note of his character to see if you two would make a good mix. See if he can make you smile. See if he, whether rich or poor, will go the extra mile just to please you. Anyone can buy you expensive bags and shoes. Anyone can take you out to five-star restaurants. Anyone can speak with proper grammar and anyone may have graduated from a university. Here is the thing, not everyone will put you first in their lives. Not everyone will possess all the characteristics of love. Not every man will make you the apple of his eye. You have to choose a spouse with your heart and not choose a spouse society thinks is ideal for you because in the end you are the one that has to go home to that person every single day of your life. Do not allow societal traditions to influence your choice of a spouse. Choose your spouse from within your heart of hearts. Choose your spouse out of love.

Number five, the Changing chapter, tells you that you should never change who you are because of what you have gone through in your past relationships. If you treated your previous spouse with love and respect yet he mistreated you, you must remember that you had nothing to do with how he treated you. In fact, it has everything to do with him. Make sure that you get into another relationship where you treat your new spouse with the same love and respect that you did in your past relationships. If you do not get over your past hurts, then I advise you to hold off from dating until you are completely over those hurts. If you are not over it, then the next person you date would find it difficult to be with you. Bringing a toxic attitude into a new relationship is a recipe for disaster.

It does not matter how beautiful and/or successful you are, if you are still bitter and hurting from your past relationships, most likely you would not give your new spouse 100 percent of yourself. Trust me, we men know when a lady is bitter, and we most definitely know when she is not giving 100 percent effort. Sadly, the average guy will be quick to walk away from a lady like this. The first part of the Love quote states that "love is patient," you have to be patient with yourself and take as much time as you need to distance yourself from your past in order for you to move on and become ready to completely give your heart to someone else. You must develop patience, which is one of the characteristics of love in order to find and keep that spouse your heart and soul desires.

Number six, the Walls chapter, talks about walls which women use indirectly, walls which push men away from them. I, at times, believe that they are unaware of their actions such as degrading men with their language, physically and/or emotionally abusing men, constant complaining and arguing, just to name a few types of walls. Some women do these kinds of things to try to control men, have power in the relationship or if they make more money than their spouse they try to show that they are superior.

Whether or not they are aware of what they are doing, the fact is that some women are pushing men away with their behavior. Men do not like a complaining woman. "Better to live on a corner of the roof than share a house with a quarrelsome wife." Proverbs 21:9. Complaining is just one of the many types of walls that I have outlined in the Wall chapter. As you can see, the fact that a man would rather live on the corner of his rooftop than to be in a warm house with his wife, speaks volumes. You have to search within yourself to see exactly what you are doing that is keeping love away from you and once you have found it, you need to get rid of it.

Most times we are our greatest enemy. We are the ones holding ourselves back. In this case, we are the ones who are guilty of preventing love from getting to us due to the walls we erected. If you are a woman who loves to complain, then you should get rid of that personality trait. It's been known that love can break down barriers. If you find someone who has the love characteristics, you will then need to destroy your walls and the habits that can potentially block him from getting to your heart.

Number seven, the Burn It chapter, talks about how you have to prepare yourself for the spouse you are looking for. Remember, make sure that you are looking for someone with the characteristics of love in their hearts. As explained in the Burn It chapter, whatever you are looking for is also looking for you. For example, if your goal is to find a man who will speak to you with respect, then you need to ask yourself a simple question, "do I speak to men with respect?" If that answer is no, then you need to burn that type of behavior. Burning your bad habits does not mean that you are changing who you are. It simply means that you are becoming a better you. Relationships are not one-sided. Both parties should be willing to go the extra mile for each other. You cannot expect your future spouse to have positive qualities while you have so many negative ones. Find out what your negative qualities are and put them on dried wood and set them on fire.

 Lastly, number eight is the Parents chapter. Parents are the first teachers for children. They do not learn from what you say. However, they learn from what you do. As parents, you have to make sure that love is exemplified throughout your home. You have to forgive your children when they do something wrong. This is how they will know what it means to forgive. You have to be slow to anger with your children. If your man does something to upset you, you should take some time to get yourself together and calm down, and then you can go and address the matter calmly with him. It is better to do it this way rather than to just go to him and yell and scream at him. As parents, you have to show love to your spouse in front of your children. Let your children see you play with your spouse. It would be good sometimes if they see their mother and father going on date nights. You must feed their innocent minds with positivity. Parents can be responsible for the directions their children take in life. It is good to make sure that your children have a good education. You also have to make sure that they know what real love is. Try your best to make sure that both you and your spouse possess the characteristics of love your children can see and learn from. They would then have a much better time finding true love in the future as well, rather than finding themselves successful, single, alone and unfulfilled.

As you can see, love is the cure-all. It is the blueprint for a healthy marriage and for life in general. Ladies, if you find a man who possesses the characteristics of love, then he is the man for you. He will not be perfect but he will be perfect for you. He may not be everything you want but he will be everything you need. You now have to make sure you possess the characteristics of love as well. I've heard of individuals going through extremely difficult times in their marriages, yet they stay together for more than 50 years. How did they stay together through those tough times you may ask? It was not because of money, or material things or even status. It was because the love they had for each other was so strong that no problem on planet earth could ever weaken their relationship.

So, if I were to ask you what kind of a man you are looking for, what answer would you give me?

AUTHOR BIO: Linton Claude Samuels was born in Jamaica, and lived there for twelve years before moving to the United States. Linton was raised in Brooklyn by his mother, her husband and sisters. For as long as he can remember, he was keenly aware of the difficulties women face in balancing careers, families, and relationships. After training as a Pharmacy Technician, Linton worked at a major metropolitan hospital in New York. A chance conversation with a nurse about the trials of her dating life led him to conceive and write Successful, Single, But... When he is not writing, Linton enjoys playing gospel and jazz piano. He is a Seventh Day Adventist Christian, and a devout church-goer. Linton is also a recipient of the Master Guide leadership award, and teaches young men discipline, wildness survival, and leadership skills.

Contact information:

Email: Lintonsamuels@gmail.com

Twitter: @lintonCSamuels

Instagram: @author_lcs

Website: www.successfulsinglebut.com

Successful, Single, But…

www.ingramcontent.com/pod-product-compliance
Lightning Source LLC
Chambersburg PA
CBHW020646230426
43665CB00008B/338